Anthony Comstock

Gambling outrages

Improving the breed of horses at the expense of public morals

Anthony Comstock

Gambling outrages
Improving the breed of horses at the expense of public morals

ISBN/EAN: 9783337145767

Printed in Europe, USA, Canada, Australia, Japan

Cover: Foto ©Andreas Hilbeck / pixelio.de

More available books at **www.hansebooks.com**

GAMBLING OUTRAGES;

OR,

IMPROVING THE BREED OF HORSES AT THE EXPENSE OF PUBLIC MORALS.

BY

ANTHONY COMSTOCK,

AUTHOR OF "FRAUDS EXPOSED," AND "TRAPS FOR THE YOUNG."

NEW YORK:
THE AMERICAN NEWS COMPANY,
AGENTS FOR THE TRADE.
1887.

PREFACE.

FOR years the laws against gambling have been openly violated.

Professional gamblers from this and other States have been permitted to go from county to county with their unlawful paraphernalia and ply their schemes of robbery, surrounded by an atmosphere filled with rumors of bribery and corruption of officials.

Public sentiment has sustained the enforcement of the laws against these dishonest schemes of getting another's property for nothing in New York and Queens Counties.

For years Kings County has unlawfully afforded gamblers opportunity to rob the people and has protected them from punishment.

A judge from the bench as far back as June, 1884, proclaimed these violations of law in Gravesend as " flagrant, persistent, and open." Still the warning has been unheeded, the laws ever since have continued to be trampled under foot, and an appeal to the public is rendered necessary. The facts published herein are published because they are *facts*. It is hoped that a full, frank, and faithful history of these outrages may promote a public sentiment strong enough to secure the rigid enforcement of laws as they now exist, and defeat the infamous attempt to repeal them in the interest of professional gamblers.

Does the Empire State belong to gamblers? Have the people no self-respect left ? Will they allow gamblers, resident and non-resident of this State, to set at defiance the

iii

laws of the State for a series of years, and then, when the demand of the people made of their servants is heard, " Let gambling cease," " Let the laws be enforced," can it be possible for gamblers to continue to rob the people and still go unwhipped of justice ? If not, then read, reflect, and act upon the facts presented in this book. The object is to secure the proper enforcement of laws against these crimes.

Honest young men or horses : which ?

ANTHONY COMSTOCK.

INTRODUCTION.

ABOVE the crime of "gambling" stands a greater, viz., the "protection of gamblers." Above the "protection of gamblers" is that cowardly silence on the part of good citizens under the endorsement of which crime and outrage become possible.

This book is designed to turn the light of historic fact on past offences committed by gamblers and officials against law, justice, public order, and public morals.

If the simple record, faithfully presented, prove distasteful to those who have failed to do their duty in the suppression of gambling crimes, let them reflect that by their wilful neglect they have contributed the· facts which make up this history.

How the Record is Made.

Affidavits, letters, records of court, or certified copies of papers, and extracts of printed matter are presented, when possible, to make the history more exact, and enable any, who are so disposed, to test the authenticity of this account of the latest and most approved methods of "improving the breed of horses" by the Kings County gambling system.

The facts are presented in the order of occurrence. Let any who may be wounded by them remember that we simply write the history made by themselves.

We do not propose to entertain the reader by reviling where we have been reviled, slandering where we have been slandered, or blackguarding where we have been blackguarded ; but only with the truth. To all the false and malicious attacks made upon us in the past we have to oppose

v

the facts. Libels, and insinuations of "blackmail," "fixed by gamblers," "silenced so they won't move," "judges and courts won't believe him under oath," etc., will be confronted with matters as they actually occurred and a faithful statement of what has been done on our part; and we believe that if the reader will but consider what is presented he will have no doubt as to the necessity of a rigid enforcement of laws against these crime-breeders, or to the fidelity and efficiency of the New York Society for the Suppression of Vice and its agents.

It is not to be expected but that this book and its author *will* be assailed by similar weapons to those used in the past; but that is no reason why it should not be written and the facts submitted to the public.

Individual interests pale before the more important interests of public morals and the future welfare of our youth.

If morals are worth preserving, and unless our youth are to grow up gamblers and thieves, the schools of vice must be closed and the gambling passion must be checked.

Reader, have we earned the right to a fair hearing? After fifteen years of faithful public service, in the face of bitter opposition, attempted assassinations, conspiracies and plots to ruin our good name and reputation, is it too much for us to ask you to spend a few hours in examining the facts concerning the non-enforcement of law against gamblers by sworn officials, especially as the facts presented are our appeal for the enforcement of laws against these crimes and our answer to the assaults made upon us by our enemies!

Above all else, the presentation of the facts is essential to the proper enforcement of law against a small army of crime-breeders. Gambling is a monster. Gambling in any form is an enemy to be dreaded in any community. It turns loose avarice and greed, unhinges common honesty, destroys industrious habits, mercilessly robs the poor, and beggars helpless women and children.

By appealing to the spirit of cupidity,—of getting some. thing for nothing,—it finds many votaries and is regarded with popular favor.

Like rum and lust, it preys upon the community, scattering misery and want along its pathway. We propose to attack this popular vice, and appeal to the reader for a verdict against it after the facts in the following pages have been considered.

THE AUTHOR.

GAMBLING OUTRAGES.

CHAPTER I.

METHODS OF PROSECUTION AND DEFENCE.

For years well known and professional gamblers have openly violated the laws of the State in Saratoga and Kings Counties.

Faro, roulette, rouge-et-noir, hazard, sweat, lottery-policy, and other banking games, all of which are felonies, together with horse pool and the like, have been conducted openly. These crimes have been persistent, flagrant, and open.

EFFORTS TO ENFORCE THE LAW.

Honest, clean, and faithful efforts have been made by the New York Society for the Suppression of Vice to enforce the laws against these demoralizing and evil practices.

These efforts have been rendered futile by sworn officials whose duty it has been to enforce these laws.

Our plans have been very simple. They have been the same as have proven very successful in other instances, and briefly stated are :

First. Good legal evidence against the criminal.

Second. Arrest the gambler and seize his gambling paraphernalia by due process of law.

Third. Bring gamblers and their traps into court, secure their conviction and sentence, followed by the destruction of their gambling apparatus.

Our efforts have been met by hostile opposition. This opposition has not come so much from gamblers whom we have endeavored to bring to justice as from sworn officers of the law, whom public rumors and the press have charged with shielding and protecting these criminals and their crimes.

Out of 113 gamblers arrested by us since May 1, 1881, followed by indictments in the Sessions Court, in Kings County, but one case has ever been convicted and sentenced in that court.

Prior to Jan. 1, 1884, Isaac S. Catlin was District Attorney. His administration of law against common gamblers indicted for felonies resulted in the dismissal of over fifty indictments during the last fifteen days of his term of office. His administration is to be credited with the conviction of one of our policy gamblers before Judge Moore, during his last term of three years. This man, William Stone, was arrested May 26, 1881, tried and convicted Feb., 1882, and yet not sentenced until Dec., 1882, and then only to a fine of $25, under the Revised Statutes, and under a statute which fixed as a minimum penalty "not less than ten days' imprisonment and $10 fine."

Four other men were convicted in the City Court of Brooklyn June, 1882, and yet none of them were sentenced throughout Mr. Catlin's term.

John Y. McKane, chief of police of Gravesend, and eight of his subordinates, policemen of that town, were indicted Sept., 1883, through our efforts, in spite of opposition to the contrary, for violating Section 349, Penal Code, and aiding and abetting gamblers. These men knowingly allowed gambling to exist, and the policemen were detailed to the betting ring to keep the purchasers of pools in line while the gambler plied his nefarious trade in violation of law.

James W. Ridgway has been District Attorney since Jan., 1884. The following history of what has *not* been done to suppress gambling will deal with his administration largely.

Early in Mr. Ridgway's term we discovered that Mr. Catlin

or his subordinates had dismissed the fifty odd indictments mentioned before. We then applied to Mr. Ridgway for the indictment of Mr. Catlin and the reindictment of these common gamblers. That made Mr. Catlin hostile to us.

We went to Mr. Ridgway soon after he came into office and assured him of our heartiest co-operation. He assured us of his intention to enforce the laws, and that he would be glad of our assistance. We believed him. Up to June, 1884, we were waiting for him to move upon our complaint against Mr. Catlin. We also were expectant concerning the other matters which were pending. As he was new in office, and it required time to straighten matters out, we did not think it strange that our cases were not brought up and disposed of. We lived on in hopes. But, as will be disclosed, in June, 1884, his sincerity was tested and his opposition was seen and felt by us.

INTEGRITY OF WITNESSES AN ELEMENT OF SUCCESS.

Let the reader bear in mind that the integrity of the witness is an essential element of success in all departments of our work.

To impeach the witness for the people is always the effort of counsel for a defendant. It is a common practice of many lawyers, especially when they have a hard case to defend, to assail the witness for the prosecution, throw mud, insinuate that the witness has been guilty of some heinous offence, or create a suspicion against him by asking "if he has not been arrested for some crime?" etc., even when they know they have no ground for such an argument. This is done to raise a doubt or awaken a prejudice in the minds of the jury, or to degrade the witness before the court. Again there is what is commonly called

"FISHING FOR EVIDENCE."

There is a little incident which will illustrate this method that occurred in one of our cases in New York City in the General Sessions Court, which also shows how sometimes "the biter gets bit."

A man had been indicted, being a common gambler, for selling a lottery policy. Mr. C. S. Spencer was defending. He went on a fishing expedition with a Mr. Van Pelt, one of our former aids. Something like the following scene occurred on cross-examination:

Mr. Spencer (very suave): Now, Mr. Van Pelt, I have one or two questions to ask you and I have done. Please speak up so that the farthest juror can hear.

Q. Where did you live before you came to New York?

A. Omaha, Nebraska.

Q. Now, sir, is it not a fact that during part of the time you were in Omaha you were in the penitentiary? (This in a very imperious manner, with a look as much as to say, "Take care, sir, what you say. I am after you.")

A. (meekly) Yes, sir.

Spencer (very exultant, with a benign look upon the jurors, and a most compassionate, "Gentlemen, I shall not detain you. I have but one or two more questions to ask this witness ") :

Q. Now, Mr. Van Pelt, just tell the jury how long you were in the penitentiary. Now, sir, speak up loud so that the farthest gentleman can hear.

A. (very subduedly) About three years.

Mr. Spencer, very exultant, with a most profound bow to the jury and most compassionate consideration, says, "Gentlemen, I shall detain you with but one more question," and turning to the witness says:

"Now, Mr. Van Pelt, I have one more question " (and as he speaks he turns toward the assistant District Attorney and the writer with a most withering look). "Now, sir, please raise your voice so all the jury can hear."

Q. What were you there for? (And Mr. Spencer posed in a most striking attitude for his reply.)

The witness without .moving a muscle of his face replied :

A. I was chief warden.

It is needless to relate that court and jury were convulsed with laughter, while Mr. Spencer dropped into his chair with a most demoralized look upon his face. He has since, many a time, laughed in the writer's presence over this incident.

These attacks upon us of our opponents are not adopted because they have any charge which can be sustained against our witnesses, but, as said before, to discredit them or to deny plain facts, or to divert public attention from some unsavory record which they of their own free will, and by neglect of official obligations, have made for themselves.

In considering the following statements of law and facts let the reader ever bear in mind that *good legal evidence was repeatedly secured against these gamblers, and placed at the disposal of the prosecuting attorneys.*

UNIMPEACHABLE WITNESSES.

Good and reliable witnesses were ever ready to appear and testify, *if they had been called by the District Attorney.* These witnesses, let it be noted, have never been impeached during the past fourteen years of our history. We have made more than 1180 arrests down to to-day. These witnesses, some of them, have been upon the witness stand hundreds of times where the utmost latitude of cross-examination has been allowed defendants and their counsel. We have had arrayed against us the dealers in obscenity and their friends, the gamblers and their fraternity, the lottery dealers and their millions, the frauds and swindlers and their scheming supporters, the so-called liberals, free-lovers, quack doctors, ex-convicts, and the National Defence

Associations, and their advocates, backed by a hostile press; and yet, notwithstanding that all these have plotted and conspired against us, and all have come into court and confronted us while we were at a disadvantage on the witness stand, under the cross fire of shrewd, acute, tricky, and often unscrupulous counsel, in pay of these opponents—yet with all their money, political intriguing, plottings, conspiracies, and insinuations not one of them has been able to lay a finger upon a single act that has impeached or would impeach these witnesses. In face of this, Mr. Ridgway, while before Governor Hill, Feb. 5, 1887, declared, in his argument to dismiss our charges there against him, that

"NO COURT WOULD BELIEVE US."

We answered him by showing that out of 75 cases brought to trial during 1886 we secured 70 convictions or pleas of "guilty." There were three disagreements secured by Mr. Ridgway for us in the Jockey Club trials of last October, and the other two cases were discharged as follows: one in New York in Special Sessions Court, a minor case; in the other, where two men were jointly indicted, the employer was convicted and sent to prison, while the accomplice, being a clerk, was acquitted.

We have dwelt upon this matter at the outset, as we have been silent under these infamous attacks so long that many will take up this work with a prejudice. We have therefore defined our position, so that we may have fair dealing and an honest judgment.

A PART OF WHAT HAS BEEN DONE.

We have secured 624 convictions, where sentences have been imposed as follows: 175 years and 10 days' imprisonment and $79,412.95 fines, while $71,700 bail-bonds have been forfeited; making a total of $151,112.95 secured for the public treasuries. We also have seized more than 45¾ tons of contraband matters.

TABULAR STATEMENT,

SHOWING A PART OF THE WORK OF THE NEW YORK SOCIETY FOR THE SUPPRESSION OF VICE.

DESCRIPTION.	Prior to January, 1886.	During 1886.	Total.
Persons arrested in U. S. Courts...... .	296	9	305†
" " " State Courts.......	712	130	842†
Discharged by committing magistrates	46	1	47
" " Juries...................	39	1	40
Convicted or plead guilty........... ..	554	70	624
Sentenced	436	64	500
Prisoners absconded...................	31	1	32
" re-arrested	37	....	37
Disagreement by Juries...............	13	3	16
Convicted on second trial.............	5	....	5
Bail-bonds forfeited.....	$67,900*	$3,800	$71,700
`	yrs. mos. days	yrs. mos. days	yrs. days.
Years of imprisonment imposed	171 5 24	3 6 16	175 10
Amount of fines imposed	$76,150.95*	$3,262	$79,412.95
Convicts pardoned....................	17	2	19
STOCK CONFISCATED.			
Books & sheet stock seized & destroyed	36,926 lbs.	....	36,926 lbs.
Obscene pictures and photos..........	233,594	1,036	234,630
Microscopic pictures for charms, knives, etc......................	7,400	....	7,400
Negative plates for making obscene photographs......................	1,767	35	1,802
Engraved steel and copper plates.....	352	....	352
Wood-cuts and electro-plates.........	544	....	544
Stereotype plates for printing books, etc........	26,423 lbs.	....	26,423 lbs.
Number of different books............	207	....	207
Lithographic stones destroyed........	50	....	50
Articles for immoral use, of rubber, etc.	91,709	191	91,900
Lead moulds for making obscene matter...........................	700 lbs.	....	700 lbs.
Establishments for making same closed	6	1	7
Indecent playing cards destroyed.....	6,122	....	6,122
Boxes of pills, powders, used by abortionists	4,210	55	4,265
Circulars, catalogues, songs, poems, etc................................	1,411,007	26,888	1,437,895
Newspapers containing unlawful advertisement or obscene matter...	22,354	....	22,354
Open letters seized in possession of persons arrested	107,461	144	107,605
Names of dealers as revealed by account books of publishers	6,000	....	6,000
Obscene pictures, framed, on walls of saloons	102	10	112
Figures & images seized and destroyed	748	....	748

* Total fines and bail forfeited, $151,112.95. † Total arrests, 1,147.

Description.	Prior to January, 1886.	During 1886.	Total.
Letters, packages, etc., seized in hands of dealers, ready for mailing at time of arrest......................	3,499 and *11 mail bags full	....	3,499 and *11 mail bags full
Names and P. O. addresses to whom circulars, etc., may be sent, that are sold as matters of merchandise, seized in hands of persons arrested.	982,220	.-......	982,220
Obscene plays stopped, or places of amusement closed..................	4	....	4
Keno layouts	1	....	1
Faro layouts	20	2	22
Roulette layouts......................	9	3	12
Rouge-et-noir layouts........	11	1	12
Lottery tickets......................	275,833	21,437	297,270
Lottery circulars....................	153,181	31,783	184,964
Lotteries suppressed.................	30	3	33
Pool tickets........	1,159,290	160,563	1,319,853
Sweat boards........................	8	....	8
Blackboards	245	59	304
Deal boxes	18	1	19
Deal trays...........................	26	1	27
Packs of cards.......................	270	7	277
Policy and pool shops raided or closed	135	51	186
Score cards—pool.....................	....	1,268	1,268
Sheets and books for recording bets..	....	947	947
Manifold-books for recording policies.	10,886	287	11,173
Gaming tables	30	6	36
Dream books	70	17	87
French pool registers.....	5	....	5
Account books........................	168	102	270
Trays for holding pool tickets	43	....	43
Ivory and composition chips..........	68,547	50	68,597
Cue boxes	8	....	8
Tally cards for faro	3,084	....	3,084
Card presses.........................	4	1	5
Prize packages.......................	2,483	....	2,483
Envelopes for envelope game..........	11,133	600	11,733
Policy slips........................	9,336	3,176	12,512
Iron safes, in gambling saloons........	7	....	7
Miles traveled by agents outside New York City........	239,530 miles.	26,900 miles.	266,430

In a word, 1,180 arrests have been made and more than 35¼ tons of obscene matter and 10½ tons of gambling material, paraphernalia, etc., have been seized and destroyed.

WE SUBMIT WE HAVE AT LEAST EARNED THE RIGHT TO BE HEARD, and that our words may be considered in this important matter.

These malicious attacks upon us but emphasize the truthfulness of the record which we present. They disprove nothing. It is, however, a matter to be inquired into by

---

* Lottery circulars.

thoughtful men that, of all those who have made attacks upon the writer of this record during the past year, in reference to these cases, it is not the gambler, not the indicted criminal, who has cause of complaint or who makes complaint, but rather it is OFFICIALS and EX-OFFICIALS, who, when good legal evidence has been brought and placed in their hands, have utterly failed to bring these criminals to justice or stop the crimes complained of. These are the ones who assail our integrity and reputation.

CHAPTER II.

RE-ELECTION OF MR. RIDGWAY.

It is said that the re-election of Mr. Ridgway, after he had neglected to enforce the laws against gamblers, is an endorsement of his conduct and a proof that what he has done is all right. Two wrongs do not make one right. The State of New York, through its Legislature, has enacted stringent laws against gambling, as will be seen below. While those laws are on the statute-book no sane person will say that any citizen or set of citizens has a right to violate them. Much less will it be said that professional gamblers, non-residents of the State of New York, have a right to come into the State and set at defiance our laws with impunity.

The re-election of Mr. Ridgway may be a source of triumph and exultation for himself and the gambling fraternity. It is not so regarded by right-thinking men.

Accepting the re-election as a fact, not stopping to argue as to how or by what influences or forces he was elected, not discussing the elasticity of the consciences of men who could, by their votes, say, " Well done, unfaithful servant; continue thou in office," let the reader calmly consider—

First, the law.

Then the duties devolving upon District Attorneys and other officials.

And then what has *not* been done under the solemn obli-
. gations of their oaths of office.

Because men, ignorant of the facts, or with a wilful intent to consent to the outrages against law, order, and justice, or at the lash of some political or gambling boss, by their **votes** have consented to or have indorsed these wrongs, does it make them right or lawful ? Manifestly, no. The Penal Code of the State of New York makes any of the following crimes a *felony*, as the penalties may be in State's prison. The Code of Criminal Procedure provides that whenever the sentence is for more than one year it must be in State's prison, and such crime a felony.

LOTTERY.

" Sec. 325. CONTRIVING, DRAWING, ETC., LOTTERY.—A person who contrives, proposes, or draws a lottery, or assists in contriving, proposing, or drawing the same, is punishable by imprisonment for not more than two years, or by a fine of not more than one thousand dollars, or both."

WHO ARE COMMON GAMBLERS ?

" Sec. 344. COMMON GAMBLER, ETC.—A person who is the owner, agent, or superintendent of a place, or of any device or apparatus for gambling; or who hires, or allows to be used, a room, table, establishment, or apparatus for such a purpose; or who engages as dealer, game-keeper, or player in any gambling or banking game, where money or property is dependent upon the result; or who sells or offers to sell what are commonly called lottery policies, or any writing, paper, or document in the nature of a bet, wager, or insurance upon the drawing or drawn numbers of any public or private lottery; or who indorses or uses a book, or other document, for the purpose of enabling others to sell, or offer to sell, lottery policies, or other such writings, papers, or documents, is a common gambler, and punishable by imprisonment for not more than two years, or by a fine not exceeding one thousand dollars, or both."

Concerning pool gambling as prohibited under Section 351 of the Penal Code, says the Supreme Court of this State, General Term at Poughkeepsie, May, 1885 :

" Sec. 351 of the Penal Code makes either of three things criminal :—
" If a person keep or occupy a place with the requisite things to record bets.
" If a person do in fact record bets.
" If an owner or occupant of premises knowingly permit the **same** to

be used for these purposes. Such acts are made misdemeanors."—People *vs.* James E. Kelly *et al.*, 37 Hun. R. p.—.

POOL GAMBLING PROHIBITED BY THE CODE.

"Sec. 351. BETS, ETC., ON HORSE RACES, ETC.—A person who keeps any room, shed, tenement, tent, booth, or building, or any part thereof, or who occupies any place upon any public or private grounds within this State, with books, apparatus, or paraphernalia, for the purpose of recording or registering bets or wagers, or of selling pools, and any person who records or registers bets or wagers, or sells pools upon the result of any trial or contest of skill, speed, or power of endurance, of man or beast, or upon the result of any political nomination, appointment, or election; or being the owner, lessee, or occupant of any room, shed, tenement, tent, booth or building, or part thereof, knowingly permits the same to be used or occupied for any of these purposes, or therein keeps, exhibits, or employs any device or apparatus for the purpose of recording or registering such bets or wagers, or the selling of such pools, or becomes the custodian or depositary, for hire or reward, of any money, property, or thing of value staked, wagered, or pledged upon any such result, is punishable by imprisonment for one year, or by fine not exceeding two thousand dollars, or both."

As showing how determined the law-makers were that these crimes should be suppressed, note the following provision of the Penal Code, requiring the seizure of all gambling paraphernalia by any person required or authorized to arrest a person for any offence against any of the foregoing sections, *and that too without a warrant.*

ON SEIZURE.

"Sec. 345. SEIZURE OF GAMBLING IMPLEMENTS AUTHORIZED.—A person, who is required or authorized to arrest any person for a violation of the provisions of this chapter is also authorized and required to seize any table, cards, dice, or other apparatus or article suitable for gambling purposes, found in the possession or under the control of the person so arrested, and to deliver the same to the magistrate before whom the person arrested is required to be taken."

NOTE, ESPECIALLY, THE DUTY OF DISTRICT ATTORNEYS, SHERIFFS, AND OTHER PEACE OFFICERS.

" Sec. 349. CERTAIN OFFICERS DIRECTED TO PROSECUTE OFFENCES UNDER THIS CHAPTER.—It is the duty of all sheriffs, constables, police officers, and prosecuting or district attorneys to inform against and prosecute all persons whom they have reason to believe offenders against the provisions of this chapter, and any omission so to do is punishable by a fine not exceeding five hundred dollars."

The " chapter " referred to is Chapter IX., Penal Code. Sections from 343 to 351 inclusive are in Chapter IX., and therefore within the provisions of Sections 345 and 349.

That the community may further comprehend the *responsibility and duty* of the District Attorney, we copy from the oath of office of James W. Ridgway, filed November 27, 1883, in the County Clerk's office of the City of Brooklyn. It is sworn to before George G. Barnard, " Deputy Clerk of the County of Kings," as follows :—

"I, James W. Ridgway, do solemnly swear that I will support the Constitution of the United States, and the Constitution of the State of New York: and that I will faithfully discharge the duties of the office of District Attorney of the County of Kings according to the best of my ability. * * * (signed) JAMES W. RIDGWAY."

On the thirtieth day of November, 1880, the same oath was filed and sworn to before the deputy clerk, Mr. George G. Barnard, by Isaac S. Catlin.

The foregoing laws existed while Mr. Isaac S. Catlin was District Attorney.

BRIGHTON BEACH CHARTER.

The Brighton Beach Racing Association of Brighton Beach filed their articles of incorporation with the Secretary of State of the State of New York, February 17, 1882. As soon as the race track was open pool gambling in the most open and bold manner commenced, under the *protection* and fostering care of local officials ; and in September, 1883, the agents of the New York Society for the Suppression of Vice caused the arrest of John Y. McKane, chief of police of the town of Gravesend, and eight of his subordinates, all of whom were indicted by the Grand Jury for "knowingly aiding and abetting" gamblers or for violation of Sections 349 and 351 of the Penal Code aforesaid. Neither McKane nor any of his subordinates have ever been tried.

THE CONEY ISLAND JOCKEY CLUB

filed their articles of incorporation at Albany, with the Secretary of State, July 3, 1879. At its race course there were more than fifty booths occupied by from two to three gamblers in each, openly violating the law. At least fifty of those same booths were occupied during the season of 1886, if the testimony of James E. Kelly, the boss gambler, who rented the privilege from the Coney Island Jockey Club, is to be believed, as given under oath in the trial of the Jockey Club before Judge Moore last October.

In reference to the facts concerning the administration of law against these crimes by Isaac S. Catlin, under his oath of office, we have simply to present the word and statement of Mr. Catlin, as made in the Brooklyn *Eagle* of October 11, 1886, without going into further details. He says :

" For five of the six years of my incumbency of the District Attorney's office pool gambling was carried on on two tracks at Coney Island, absolutely without complaint from any source. I concede that I did not during these five years, during which everybody seemed to acquiesce in the matter, take any steps towards stopping pool selling. Mr. Comstock will likely at once condemn this as a gross violation of his favorite Section 349, of the Penal Code, and will proceed to explain its wickedness to the Committee on Investigation."

The record speaks for itself and carries with it its own condemnation. We simply desire to assure the reader that his statements are true, that the laws were openly violated, and that he did not take any effectual steps towards stopping the violations of law. His oath of office may not have much of any value with the public now, but his word is correct about this. We simply contribute our mite towards establishing him in the truth in this respect at least.

The statement that "everybody acquiesced" is not true. The crimes were denounced by different papers in 1882 and 1883, particularly *The Union* and New York papers, while they were frequently complained of to Mr. Catlin by the representatives of this Society.

But as Mr. Catlin has retired to private life, and has not the enforcement of the law against these criminals in his hands, it is proposed to leave him with his record, offering our services, at any time in the future he may require, to confirm him whenever he shall attempt to present a faithful record of his doings to the community, especially in matters where we know he is telling the truth. Which is the weaker, Mr. Catlin's "oath" or the "best of his ability"?

The following synopsis will illustrate his respect for his oath of office and the duties imposed upon him by Section 349, which he treats so flippantly, and also his "best ability."

MR. CATLIN'S RECORD.

Total number of indictments found against gamblers during 1881, 1882, and 1883 - - - - - - - - - - 97
Total number of persons tried and convicted - - - - 5
Total number of persons sentenced after conviction - - - 1
Total number of indictments improperly dismissed, during the last ten days of Catlin's term - - - - - - - 57
Total indictments remaining untried (on some of which the defendants never pleaded) - - - - - - - 34

These figures are taken from the testimony of Messrs. Catlin and Ridgway as given before the Bacon Investigating Committee in March, 1887.

We require no better witness to prove the maladministration of law against gambling during Mr. Catlin's terms than his own witness, Isaac S. Catlin.

WHAT PRINCIPLES OF LAW AND GOVERNMENT ARE VIOLATED BY THESE UNLAWFUL GAMBLING GAMES?

Some one will say: "What! do you object to gentlemen betting between themselves upon a horse race? Why, that is fanatical!" I reply that that question is not involved. The question of two individuals betting between themselves is not embraced under this statute nor in this discussion. The right of any two gentlemen to make a bet between themselves may be a matter of taste, and should not be confused with the only question involved in the administration of law under Section 351, to wit: May professional gamblers defy the laws of this State, violate the fundamental principles of government, and, in defiance of decisions at Common Law and the Court of Appeals to the contrary, set up their gambling paraphernalia in the midst of multitudes of pleasure seekers, and in "persistent, flagrant, and open" violation of stringent law to the contrary rob and plunder the public? That is the question, and the only question. It is a

FUNDAMENTAL PRINCIPLE OF GOVERNMENT

that a person shall not be deprived of his money or property without a just and fair equivalent.

Says that eminent jurist, Judge Catron, whose opinions, delivered from the supreme bench both of the State of Tennessee and of the nation, will ever be regarded as of the highest authority, in the celebrated case of "The State *vs.* Smith & Lane" (2 Yer. Tenn. R.):

"The presumption of law is that every man has acquired his property honestly; and it is the policy of every well-regulated government that he

shall not be deprived of it without a fair equivalent. This is particularly
the case in Republics, where all should be independent in the means of
subsistence."

In the same case this learned Judge paints a picture of
the effects of gaming which may well be considered at this
time. He says:

" Gaming is a general evil, leads to vicious inclinations, destruction of
morals, abandonment of industry and honest employments, a loss of
self-control and respect. Frauds, forgeries, thefts, make up the black
catalogue of crime, the closing scene of which generally ends in highway
robbery or murder. The American and European journals are full of cases
of the most distressing nature of bankers, merchants, clerks of banking
institutions, men in almost every department of trust, public and private,
becoming bankrupts and thieves, to the ruin of themselves and others.
Look for the source of their misfortune; you find it in lotteries, loo,
faro, thimble, dice, and *the like.*"

Under Common Law gambling *per se* was not indictable,
and yet " *the keeping of a common gambling house* " or place
for the public to gamble was indictable.

Says the Court of Appeals of the State of New York, concerning pool gambling :

" The evident intention of the Legislature was to discourage and repress
gambling in all its forms, including bets and wagers and every species of
wager contracts of hazard, as a great public mischief calling for ef-
fective measures of prevention and remedy."—(Ruckman *vs.* Pitcher,
1 N. Y. page 450.)

In this connection let it be remembered that this system of
"improving the breed of horses," as it is now erroneously
styled by its advocates, mortgages a large number of voters to
the gambling fraternity. It gives unscrupulous men an opportunity to put the thumb of blackmail upon their struggling
victims. The young clerk, crazed by the hope of gain, steals
from his employer. He stakes all and loses. In his desperation he goes to the gambler, begging him to return his
money, and oftentimes places himself entirely within the

2

control of the gambler by confessing his guilt. The confession of guilt is made as a plea to the gambler to give up his ill-gotten gain, that the clerk may return the stolen funds; but, instead of giving it up, many are the cases where the confession is held as a terror over the victim's head and he is made to do the gambler's bidding. Many a suicide follows the treachery of these unscrupulous robbers.

POLITICAL REASONS.

From a political standpoint these crimes have no place in any Republic or civilized community. No words seem more appropriate in this connection than to repeat the words of that eminent jurist already referred to (Catron), where, in the foregoing case cited, he uses the following language, which ought to be considered as words of warning by every thoughtful citizen. He says:

" Reduce a man to want, by gaming or otherwise, and he is no longer free to exercise the elective franchise, but dependent upon the hand that furnishes himself and family with bread. Not only ruin and beggary, but drunkenness, are almost uniformly the effect of gaming. The two vices combined are more likely to sap the foundation of our institutions than all others put together. Destroy freedom of thought and independence of action in voting at primary elections of the people, and the idea of governing by majorities is a farce, the popular will a delusion, bowing to the dictation of the wealthy minority."

From a PATRIOTIC STANDPOINT he says:

" The patriot, anxious for the prosperity of his country and the durability of her institutions, repines at the thought of seeing the haggard, hungry, and naked gamblers, or the besotted drunkard, dragged to the polls and forced to vote at the beck of his, I might almost say, master, and he a champion of the loo table or faro bank. In pecuniary means a political power, knavery rises upon the ruins of honesty and independence. Wheresoever in these Republics gaming is in any shape tolerated, pauperism, supported by the government, is in nine instances out of ten the consequence of it and its kindred vice, drunkenness.''

MORAL STANDPOINT.

From a moral standpoint this eminent jurist speaks no less earnestly and emphatically ; and no words that I can command, and no legal authority of the hundreds bearing upon this subject could be weightier or more important as words of warning than his when he says, in speaking of the gambling passion :

" Like other passions which agitate the great mass of the community, it lies dormant until once aroused, and then, with the contagion and fury of a pestilence, it sweeps morals, motives to honest pursuits and industry into the vortex of vice, unhinges the principles of religion and common honesty; the mind becomes ungovernable, and is destroyed to all useful purposes ; chances to successful gambling alone are looked to for prosperity in life, even for the daily means of sustenance ; trembling anxiety for success in lotteries, at the faro bank or loo table exclude all other thoughts. Expectation is disappointed; more losses are sustained ; . . . . swindling, forgery, theft, every crime that extreme necessity and outcast desperation can suggest to men lost to all moral ties, though guarded against, are likely shortly to follow in the train."

Under the head of " Special Arguments " in favor of this system of "improving the breed of horses " will be found instances from life supporting this wonderful description of the effect of the monster evil—gambling.

INDUSTRIOUS HABITS.

But this learned Judge does not stop here ; he goes farther and shows its *effects* upon *industrious habits.* He says :

" Gaming in any and every shape lays itself at the root of industrious habits. Where is the man, or the woman, who will labor at home or abroad patiently to earn a few shillings by the day, when excited by the hope of winning $10,000, or $100,000 in a lottery ? All rest in anxious expectation of the highest or a very high prize. Where is the professional man or mechanic who will toil at his vocation and acquire by shillings, when his mind is diseased by similar hopes ? We know he abandons his calling, and relies upon gambling chances for his own and his family's support; the man is a vagrant in mind, and must beg, swindle, steal, or starve."

Says the " Encyclopædia Americana," Vol. III., under Gambling : *

" In England, at common law, it was held a common gambling house, kept for lucre or gain, was *per se* a common nuisance, as it tends to draw together idle and evil-disposed persons, *to corrupt their morals* and ruin their fortunes ; being the same reasons given in the case of houses of common prostitution."— (King *vs.* Rogers and Humphreys.)

Does pool gambling as conducted at Coney Island and Saratoga draw together idle and evil-disposed persons to the corruption of their morals ?

" In the United States, the keeping of a common gambling house is indictable at common law on account of its *evil influence on public morals.*" —(1 Bish. Crim. Law, 504; 1 Rus. 3 Eng. Ed. 325 ; U. S. *vs.* Dixon, 4 Cran. Jr. C. C. 107; State *vs.* Savannah, T. W. P. Charl. 235; State *vs.* Doon, R. M. Charl. 1.)

Again, on page 181, in speaking of the odds against the gambler's victim, it says :

" Adroitness, cunning, experience at manipulating cards, sleight-of-hand, skill, and practice in trickery, robbery by trick and device, a keen knowledge of human nature and the weakness of mankind when aroused by greed, contend against ignorance, folly, blinded hopes, cloud ed judgment, and often distress, desperation, and a brain fired and unbalanced by the wine-cup."

COMMON LAW.

The Common Law principle, upon which " common gambling houses " are indictable, is notoriously violated when the pool gamblers at the Coney Island Jockey Club, Brighton Beach, Saratoga, or any other race track in this State, are permitted to set up their gambling paraphernalia in the

---

* Supplement to " Encyclopædia Britannica."

midst of throngs of people and there exert their demoralizing influences upon mixed assemblies.

It cannot be denied that the effect upon the minds of
many a youth is bewildering in the extreme ; that the excitement, magnetism, and pressure of the crowd, the eager
expectancy and hope of winning, and the general rush and
excitement of the throng, with the enticing odds offered, and
invitations of the gambler " to come up and bet," all serve
to push the poor victim beyond his resources, until judgment is displaced by the eager expectation of what he may
receive, and moral restraint gives way to disappointment,
desperation, and anxious hope.

CHAPTER III.

WHO THE GAMBLERS ARE.

IN view of the individual, political, patriotic, loyal, and moral reasons given why this scourge should be abated, it will be of interest to consider

WHO ARE THE GAMBLERS.

It is well for the people to know who it is that violates the law with immunity from punishment. Who are the gamblers who, residing outside of the city of Brooklyn, have more control in the administration of the affairs of Kings County than resident law-abiding citizens have, who have a monopoly of violating laws, and who have the power and the influence, year after year, to say : " The laws of the State of New York against gambling shall not be enforced in Kings County " ?

WHO ARE THE GAMBLERS IN KINGS COUNTY?

In Kings County, at the Coney Island Jockey Club race track, there were last season, and for years past, men from Pennsylvania, Maryland and New Jersey, to say nothing of the rank and file from some of the leading gambling saloons in the city of New York. James E. Kelly testified before Judge Moore's court last October, that he rented the fifty booths of the Coney Island Jockey Club for the season. But he did not tell (indeed, he was not asked the question by Mr. Ridgway, who examined him) whether he knew that each one of these booths paid the Jockey Club for the purpose of gambling $100 an afternoon (or a total of $5000). This $100 each afternoon was paid for the use of a booth

four feet square, with a table and two chairs that, at the outside, could not have cost more than $10.

March 19, 1887, before the Bacon Legislative Investigating Committee, James E. Kelly swore that the largest
amount he ever paid the Coney Island Jockey Club was
$5100 per day, and that he had taken in "as much as fifty
thousand dollars in a day " (page 511, Report) from French
and auction pools. When asked what portion of the booths
he occupied when he took in this sum, he declared : " I had
charge of the auction and French pools at that time."
John Y. McKane, chief of police, also swore that he con-
structed the booths, and that they were each about *four feet
square.* Just think of it : $100 per day for a space four feet
square !

James E. Kelly has been for more than twenty years a
gambler. He is known as " Kelly & Bliss," of 15 West
Twenty-eighth Street, and formerly was located at Long
Island City, where in October, 1882, he was indicted, and
upon search warrants issued by the Honorable Jasper S.
Gilbert, then justice of the Supreme Court, his place was
effectually raided, the paraphernalia seized, and he and his
crew driven out of that city. It will be remembered that
during 1881 and 1882 the better class of citizens of Queens
County endeavored to dislodge the gamblers from their
stronghold in that county. A Law and Order Society was
formed. They appealed to the sheriff and to the local authorities, but appealed in vain. It was found that these officials
were subjugated to the gamblers' will, and that the gamblers
had more control over them than the citizens who demanded
the enforcement of the law.

The Law and Order Society appealed to the New York
Society for the Suppression of Vice for assistance. We
secured the evidence, and on the 9th day of October, 1882,
raided four notorious places known as " Kelly & Bliss,"
"Johnson & Co.," " William Lovell," and " White & Co."

Dislodged from Queens County, these gamblers then went to Kings County, where ever since, under the fostering care and protection of local authorities, they have been permitted to violate the law with immunity from punishment.

James E. Kelly was arrested May, 1884, in New York, by the agents of the Society for the Suppression of Vice, for recording bets at Jerome Park. June 16, 1884, he pleaded "guilty" in Special Sessions Court, and was fined $100 for said offence. Two of his assistants, known as Thomas Murray and John S. Stow, also pleaded "guilty" the same day in the same court, and each was fined. After paying their fines these men went over to Kings County and violated the same laws; and the same afternoon the agents of the New York Society for the Suppression of Vice secured the evidence against them, and afterwards caused them to be indicted for said offences, as will be more clearly seen a little farther on. Daniel Gleason is also known as a partner, or employé of James E. Kelly, and was also indicted at the same time for an offence committed June 16, 1884, in Kings County.

Michael Murray was also before the Special Sessions Court, New York City, June 16, 1884, at the same time that Kelly and his men pleaded. He had been arrested for a like offence at Jerome Park. On motion of his counsel his case was set over till Oct., 1884, when he and his two pals, James Varly and Daniel Wartzfelder, each pleaded "guilty" and were each sentenced to pay a fine.

The three men last named were also, the same afternoon (June 16, 1884), violating the law again at Sheepshead Bay, and were subsequently indicted for said offences in Kings County upon our complaints.

Michael Murray is better known as "Big Mike" Murray, boss gambler, of No. 19 West Twenty-eighth Street, New York City, where he is also known as "Murray & Cridge," and "Cridge & Company," and also "Cridge & Co.," No. 56

New Street.   In this man's establishment in New York, June, 1884, we seized three roulette wheels and layouts, three faro-banks and layouts, three poker tables, one sweat table, 100 dice, 80,000 pool tickets, fifteen blackboards, etc.

John T. McDougall, of Hoboken, N. J., ran a gambling booth at Sheepshead Bay.   He is said to be a brother of the notorious Dougal McDougall who was formerly arrested as the Tattersall Turf Club, of No. 43 Broadway, New York City.   Dougal endeavored to protect his unlawful business there by swearing out an injunction restraining the writer from interfering with him, on the ground that there was nothing unlawful carried on, and that we proposed to inter-fere with his lawful and legitimate calling, etc.   This was in July, 1882.

As he is to figure prominently as a willing tool of Mr. Ridgway's and the gamblers' in this book, a little insight into his character will be of interest.

In securing his injunction he swore, according to a copy which his counsel served upon us in a proceeding had in the Supreme Court, as follows :

TATTERSALL'S TURF CLUB, }
    vs.   }
ANTHONY COMSTOCK. }

 City and County of New York, ss.

 Dougal McDougall, being duly sworn, says :

 " That the plaintiff's organization is entirely a private organization, so far as the public is concerned.   That the public are at no time admitted to the rooms of the plaintiff, and are at no time permitted to avail themselves of the privileges thereof."

Notwithstanding the above, this place, before we raided it, was thronged daily with the betting fraternity.   He further swears:

 " That no betting or gambling of any kind is permitted in the rooms of the plaintiff, *and none has ever taken place there, nor would the same be tolerated therein.*"

He also further swore in another place, and we ask careful attention to what he swears to, to wit :—

"In no way keeps, hires, or occupies any room, or rooms, with apparatus or paraphernalia for the purpose of receiving or registering bets or wagers, or sells for money pools upon the result of trials or contests of speed of horses. (Signed) D. McDOUGALL."

This was dated July 25, 1882, and on the same date an injunction was served upon us.

Our agents had previously been into this place, and had secured most absolute evidence against McDougall and his unlawful business. He kept one of the most extensive gambling establishments for selling pools and recording bets and wagers that then existed anywhere. Honest John McKean was then District Attorney. The matter was brought to his notice. He took our witnesses immediately before the learned and beloved Recorder of New York City. Warrants and search warrants were issued and, notwithstanding the injunction, Dougal McDougall was arrested, and about quarter of a million pool tickets were seized in the premises which he swore so glibly about as aforesaid. There was also found there a large number of blackboards and other gambling paraphernalia.

Dougal was indicted. Afterwards he pleaded guilty to two indictments, was sentenced on one, and sentence suspended on the other, pending his good behavior. This man of elastic conscience is the one whom Mr. Ridgway found so willing to aid him in a little scheme to befog the public mind and manufacture capital against the Society's efforts to secure the enforcement of the law against Coney Island gamblers, as will more fully appear hereafter.

William Lovell, another boss gambler, has places in Philadelphia, New Jersey, and New York City. He has been convicted in New Jersey. He was one of the boss gamblers at Queens County in 1882, and was also indicted and successfully driven out from Long Island City at the time of the celebrated raid made upon the gamblers in October, 1882, by the agents of the New York Society for the Suppression of Vice.

Martin Jordan, alias Mark Jordan, is the reputed partner of Lovell at 39 West Twenty-eighth Street, New York City.

W. H. Johnson is another boss gambler, known as "W. H. Johnson & Co.," of Sheepshead Bay, and "Johnson & Co.," Long Island City, with headquarters also in New York. David J. Johnson, known as "Johnson & Applebee," is also another boss gambler who has been repeatedly arrested.

James Dunn resides at Fairview, N. J. He had charge of the French pool at Sheepshead Bay.

Alfred H. Cridge, of Philadelphia, is presumed to be the partner of "Big Mike" Murray. These men are regarded as among the first book-makers or pool gamblers of the country.

The Coney Island Jockey Club, of New York City, own and control the race course at Sheepshead Bay, in the town of Gravesend.

Among the charter members and managers of this club are, Leonard Jerome, P. S. Forbes, John G. Heckscher, Thomas M. Foote, Eugene M. Jerome.

The active officials last year were J. G. K. Lawrence and A. W. Sanford.

These men gamble? Oh, no! Preposterous to even suspect it of them! They only allow James E. Kelly, "Big Mike" Murray, Lovell, Johnson, Cridge, McDougall & Co. to manage this branch of "improving the breed of horses," provided each booth, of the fifty or more, pays the club at least $100 per afternoon each race day.

The advocates of this science of cultivating horseflesh declare that "if pool gambling is stopped horse-racing will be ruined." It is claimed that the " poor " men aforesaid, who compose the club, cannot *afford* to keep up the races without the help and assistance of the gamblers' profits.

In other words, the jockey clubs are practically in this position : If gamblers can be permitted to plunder the people by their gambling schemes in violation of law, and then divide their ill-gotten gains with them, they will race horses.   .

Gen. Daniel Butterfield, one of the directors of the Coney Island Jockey Club, May 23, 1887, while before Governor Hill advocating the passage of the infamous Ives Pool Bill, used as an argument in behalf of this bill the fact that his club had received since the club started in 1879 the sum of $1,144,000, and had paid out this entire amount to horse owners.

He produced papers to show that the first year his club received over $81,000. In 1885 over $225,000, and in 1886 over $237,000. He did not, however, show how much of these immense sums each year had been made up from embezzlements, defalcations, thefts, robberies, and breaches of trust committed by the gamblers' victims. He did not show how many homes had been wrecked, how many families beggared, how many characters had been ruined in order to enable the gamblers to turn over the hundreds of thousands of dollars, which they do annually, of blood money, for the benefit of his club, so that his club might furnish the foundation of the scheme by which the gambler might rake in the shekels of the weak and unwary. It is the general public that are taxed for the benefit of horse owners, and this tax is collected by the gambling booths at the race track and paid over to the Jockey Club, and this, too, utterly regardless of what the effects upon public morals may be.

" Horse owners " is a very indefinite term. It embraces members of the club, gamblers, etc., and is principally made up of those who have a direct connection or interest in the success of the gamblers' schemes.

WHAT GAMBLERS MUST DO EACH DAY.

What does it cost each booth to improve the breed of horses by this Kings County system ?
Let us illustrate. Note the following bill of expenses :

James E. Kelly, boss gambler :
To expenses of running one 4x4 booth at the Sheepshead Bay race course.

DR.

To rent Coney Island Jockey Club one afternoon............$100 00
To salaries of three men to attend booth daily, $10 each....... 30 00
To car fare for three men and return to New York, daily, 40 cts.   1 20
To lunch and incidental expenses, three men.................   5 00

Total expenses each race day....................$136 20

As has been shown, more than $5000 per day is paid for rent alone. Multiply the total expense by 50 and we find that the modest amount of $6,810.00 is required to be taken out of the public by the gamblers each afternoon before they can turn a dollar's profit to themselves. This club runs 20 days each year—$6,810 by 20=$136,200. The public must pay this large amount for the gamblers' expenses. Does any one suppose these gentry labor for the poor horse without pay ? or that they are allowed to openly violate the law without paying some one roundly for its privilege and protection ? No one is so simple-minded.

At Brighton Beach the Brighton Beach Racing Association appear to control this horse-improving system themselves. The charter members are named in their charter as follows :

Wm. A. Engeman, Wm. H. Stillwell, C. J. Bergen, James McGowan, Geo. S. Mackenzie, Howard Fitzpatrick, and Joseph McMahon.

The managers last year were such horse-wise and enthusiastic breeders as Geo. H. Engeman, vice-president and manager, and A. H. Battersby, superintendent and cashier.

March 26, 1887, one Mitchell, a former clerk of this association, swore, before the Bacon Legislative Investigating Committee, that there were eight French registering machines for recording pools, and that they received as high as $80,000 per day from this source on this race course. In 1884 they had more than 125 days of improving the breed of horses by this system.

The fraternity aforesaid are the ones in whose interests the laws are abrogated—the ones who have such powerful and subtle influence as to continue to violate the law of the State year after year, and so paralyze the arm of justice that it cannot reach them. They have treated courts, Legislature, and law-abiding citizens with contempt.

What is the meritorious element of the gambling business that places its adherents above laws and justice? A full answer may be found in the fact that they divide their ill-gotten gains with the " poor " jockey-club men, who, in return therefor are willing to improve the breed of horses at the expense of law, order, and public morals.

The horse race is a basis for the gambler's traffic.

Prior to 1885 efforts had repeatedly been made to license these crimes.

In 1885 a petition, signed by a number of prominent men in Brooklyn and New York, was sent to the Legislature, practically brazenly asking them to "improve the breed of horses " by allowing gamblers to ply their traffic for 60 days each year upon each agricultural fair ground and race track in the State.

Some of the facts found in Chapter XII. on " Special Arguments " were presented to the Legislature, and this petition and effort in the interest of gamblers failed.

Again, in 1887, the same bill was introduced by Assemblyman Finn, and referred to the Judiciary Committee of the Assembly, where it received an adverse report.

Not to be outdone, February 25, 1887, Assemblyman Ives introduced another bill, which contained very peculiar provisions. It was introduced, as is stated, on behalf of the American and Coney Island Jockey Clubs, and was entitled :

" An Act to provide for the taxation of racing associations, and to prescribe the period each year during which racing may take place upon the grounds of associations incorporated for the purpose of improving the breed of horses."

SEC. 1 provides a tax of 5 per cent. upon the gross receipts for admission to any race course, to be paid to the Comptroller of the State before the 15th day of December each year.

Provided, that all associations within 20 miles of New York or Brooklyn shall be taxed not less than $4000, except in the case of such associations as shall confine themselves to holding trotting races, when it shall be $1000, and these taxes, whatever they be, must be paid each year before the first day of April.

Generous souls, these, to go to the Legislature and petition that they may be taxed to improve the breed of horses ! Why not make a voluntary contribution without an Act of the Legislature, if they are so very zealous for the poor horse ?

But in order that the poor horse shall not get cheated, Section 2 obliges every president and treasurer of each association to make a report to the comptroller, before the 15th day of November of each year, of the gross receipts. This report must be under oath.

Then, to make it doubly sure that the horse is not defrauded, in case his professed friends become lukewarm or neglectful, Section 3 authorizes the comptroller to examine their books, fix and determine the amount of tax, and collect the same.

Section 5 then provided that the revenues thus received and collected by the comptroller shall be annually disbursed on behalf of the State for prizes for improving the breed of "cattle, sheep, and horses at the various State and county fairs," all under the direction of the governor.

Political jugglery and gambling intriguing combined! This is a sop to the farmers of the State and to country members of the Legislature. They would have it appear that there is a bonanza ahead for stock-raisers. This all looks plausible and very persuasive. Magnificent liberality! The advocates of this bill desire the law-makers of the State to oblige them to be thus taxed, for the benefit of improving "cattle, sheep, and horses." But sad to say, Section 4 contains the "nigger in the fence," as appears in the following words, to wit:

"And the provisions of Section 351, Penal Code, shall not apply to the grounds of such associations during the thirty days in each year during which the said races are hereby authorized."

Not one word about improving the morals of the community. Not a cent for improving the rank and file of our young men. Not a dollar towards encouraging honesty, morality, and fair dealing for farmers' sons. But, rather, a purse for a county fair to offer for improved sheep, cattle, and horses, provided the professional gambler of this and other States may have the privilege of fleecing the unwary and impoverishing the poor by their gambling schemes of robbery. The Coney Island Jockey Club of Sheepshead Bay to pay a tax of $4000, each year, provided Section 351 is suspended, so that professional gamblers may be permitted to plunder the public on their grounds, and pay them $5000 *per day* out of the blood money. What a monstrosity!

CHAPTER IV.

WHAT HAS BEEN DONE?

WHAT HAS NOT BEEN DONE?

IN the presence of law, official obligation, and oath of office, political, patriotic, and moral considerations, what has been done in Kings County to prevent the wide-spread pestilence of pool and other gambling games? The New York Society for the Suppression of Vice answers:

"We have, year after year, secured legal evidence against professional gamblers openly violating the law; we have endeavored to apply the same remedies that have proven effectual in hundreds of other cases; and yet our efforts have been thwarted by those whose solemn duty it has been, and now is, to enforce these laws."

Year after year these officials have wilfully taken it upon themselves to prevent the punishment of these gamblers, and to hinder this organization from applying the usual remedy, to wit: "*the punishment of the gambler*, and *the destruction of his unlawful paraphernalia*" from going into effect.

CONSIDERATIONS.

The question will be asked, What are the considerations greater than the welfare of the community, the defence of the principles of our institutions of free government, obedience to the command of the law, the protection of public order and morals, and the binding obligation of the oath of office, which can possibly be presented to District Attorneys and courts to induce them to sacrifice every principle of patriotism and morality involved, in order to perpetuate, de-

3

fend, and *shield from punishment* these criminals and their crimes ?

Read the following facts, and then say whether or no the demand that these gambling crimes cease, and that these professional gamblers be punished, shall remain longer unanswered. Consider the outrages against law, order, and public morals, the scandal upon the administration of justice, and the shameful contempt put upon the courts in the past by these lawless gamblers.

STATEMENT OF FACTS.

Mr. James W. Ridgway was waited upon early in January, 1884, and assured of the hearty co-operation of the New York Society for the Suppression of Vice and its agents. His attention was called to the fact that a large number of indictments against gamblers were then pending in his office. He professed great sincerity of purpose, requested the writer to procure a list of all the indictments then remaining untried, promised to give the same prompt consideration and have the parties called and prosecuted. It was while examining this list of untried cases that we discovered that more than fifty indictments had been dismissed during the last month of Mr. Isaac S. Catlin's administration. A report was made in affidavit form to Mr. Ridgway on the 10th day of February, 1884, which paper was personally delivered to him on that day, as follows :—

(COPY.)

CITY OF BROOKLYN,
COUNTY OF KINGS,   } ss.
AND STATE OF NEW YORK.

Anthony Comstock, of 150 Nassau Street, New York City, being duly sworn, deposes and says that he is Secretary and Chief Special Agent of the New York Society for the Suppression of Vice. That he has just cause to believe, and verily does believe, that Isaac S. Catlin was District Attorney in and for the County of Kings during the years 1881, 1882, and

1883. That in the spring of 1881 Isaac S. Catlin, then District Attorney, sent for deponent and informed deponent that Governor Cornell (then Governor of the State of New York) had issued a proclamation calling upon the District Attorney and others to enforce the laws against lottery and policy gambling. That he, the said Catlin, was anxious to enforce the laws in his district, but that upon examining certain indictments against said lottery and policy gamblers, then in his office as District Attorney, he found they were not supported by legal evidence. The said Isaac S. Catlin did then request deponent to secure the proof and evidence against those who were violating the laws against lottery and policy gambling in the city of Brooklyn and cause the arrest of persons so offending; that he, the said Catlin, would prosecute them according to law.

Deponent further says that on the 26th day of May, 1881, he again visited Isaac S. Catlin, and laid before him the complaints, duly drawn with the exhibits attached thereto, against twenty-six persons charged with selling what is commonly called lottery policies. That the said Isaac S. Catlin did then and there examine the said complaints and evidence, and advised the arrest of all the parties. That twenty-one of the said parties were arrested, and indicted by the Grand Jury. That afterward, to wit, on or about the dates placed to the left of the names on the annexed paper marked Exhibit "A," the following persons were arrested, and on the dates placed to the right of their names were indicted for violating the laws of the State of New York prohibiting the sale of lottery policies. That the following memorandum, also placed opposite the names on the said paper, designates the disposition of said indictments by the District Attorney. That upon all of the said indictments the said Isaac S. Catlin as District Attorney did unlawfully omit and fail to prosecute. That all of said indictments were supported by legal evidence, and as deponent is informed and verily believes, sufficient evidence to convict if the persons indicted had been properly prosecuted by the said District Attorney at the time.

Deponent further says that Henry Dela Motta and Abraham Dela Motta, while said indictments were pending against them, were again arrested in March, 1883, and indicted in June, 1883, for additional violation of law, and deponent says that the said Isaac S. Catlin did unlawfully omit and fail to prosecute the said Abraham Dela Motta and Henry Dela Motta, and as deponent is informed and believes, upon the last named indictments against the said Dela Motta, that the said Isaac S. Catlin as District Attorney did utterly omit and fail to prosecute, and that the prisoners were not even arraigned to plead upon the said indictments, as the indictments now show.

EXHIBIT " A."

Date of Arrest.	Name of Policy Gambler.	Date of Indictment.	Disposition of Indictment.
May 26, 1881.	Charles W. Smith	June 21, '81, and Oct. 28, '81	4 Indictments dismissed December 31, 1883.
" "	Andrew McClellan	June 21, 1881	1 " " " "
" "	William Stone	Oct. 28, 1881	3 " " " "
" "	Charles Stange	June 21, '81, and Oct. 11, '81	2 " " " 29, "
" "	John L. Walker	June 21, 1881	4 " " " 30, "
" "	Simeon Cryer	June 21, Oct. 10, Oct. 28, '81	3 " " " 22, "
" "	Henry Dela Motta	June 21, Oct. 11, 1881	2 " " " 31, "
" "	Edward McEvoy	June 21, 1881	3 " " " 31, "
" "	William Lauer	June 21, 1881	2 " " " 29, "
" "	John Shubert	June 21, 1881	3 never tried. Died Feb., 1882.
" "	Christopher Bantle	June 21, 1881	2 dismissed December 31, 1883.
" "	James G. Roe	June 21, 1881	3 " " " 29, "
" "	Thomas Laird	June 21, and Oct. 10, 1881	2 " " " "
" 30, "	Michael Carney	Oct. 10, 1881	3 " " " 26, "
" "	Abraham Dela Motta	Oct. 10, 1881	2 " " " 29, "
" "	William Steiner	Oct. 10, 1881	2 " " " 31, "
" "	Thomas Ricker		" " " 31, "
" "	Edward Mayers		
Oct. 18,	John Shelter	Nov. 22, 1881	1 Indictment dismissed December 31, 1883.
" "	John Funk	Nov. 22, 1881	1 " " " "
Dec. 2,	John Mangin	Dec. 9, 1881	1 " " " 22, "
" 5,	William Rose	Oct. 10, 1881, Jan. 9, 1882	2 " " " 22, "
March, 1883.	Carl Fuller	Oct. 12, 1881, Jan. 9, 1882	2 " " " 29, "
" "	Abraham Dela Motta	June, 1883	" " " 22, "
" "	Henry Dela Motta		Never arraigned to plead to indictment.
" "	Peter Vanderhorf	Oct. 9, 1882	2 Indictments dismissed December 29, 1883.
" "	Catherine Vanderhorf		2 " " " 22, "
" "	Walter Foster	Sept. 28, 1883	1 " " " 29, "
" "	Andrew J. Philips (alias David).		2 " " " 22, "
Dec. 5,	Elizabeth Kepple	Sept. 28, 1883	1 Pending before committing magistrate.
" "	Carl Fuller	Oct. 9, 1882	2 " "
" "	Robert Johnson		" "
" "	Catherine Fitziiman		" "

Deponent further says that he is informed, and believes, that in each of the aforesaid cases there was full and ample evidence to convict the aforesaid named persons as common gamblers and for violating the laws of the State of New York, prohibiting the sale of what are commonly called lottery policies. That if the said Isaac S. Catlin had lawfully prosecuted the said persons so arrested and indicted for said offence as aforesaid, there was ample evidence to have convicted in each case, and especially in the cases against Abraham Dela Motta and Henry Dela Motta.

Deponent further says, that he is informed and verily believes that indictments against all of the aforesaid named persons were dismissed on the days and dates as follows :

December 22, indictments were dismissed charging the following persons with selling lottery policies, to wit: Theodore Fuller, alias Carl Fuller, 3 indictments; John L. Walker, 2 indictments; John Funk, 1 indictment; Michael Carney, 2 indictments; John Mangin, 1 indictment.

December 26, three indictments dismissed against Thomas Laird.

December 29, two indictments against Christopher Bantle, also two indictments against Peter Vanderhorf, and one indictment against Walter Foster and Andrew J. Phillips; one indictment against William Stone; two indictments against James G. Roe; two indictments against Elizabeth Kepple; three indictments against William Rose; three indictments against John McEvoy and Edward McEvoy each; on December 31, 1883, four indictments against Simeon Cryer; two indictments against Henry Dela Motta, and two againt Abraham Dela Motta; three indictments against Andrew McClellan; two indictments against John Shubert; two indictments against Charles Stange; five indictments against Charles W. Smith; two indictments against William Steiner, and one indictment against John Shelter.

Deponent further says, that the said Isaac S. Catlin did utterly omit and fail to prosecute Walter Foster and Andrew J. Phillips, charged with selling lottery policies ; that the evidence in these cases consists of the numbers, or what is commonly called lottery policy, sold by the said Foster and Phillips, and, further, the testimony of a witness who saw them sell the said lottery policy and record the same on a manifold book, and besides this, the manifold-books upon which the plays were recorded were found in the possession of each of the defendants, Foster and Phillips.

Deponent further says, that the said Phillips was at the time of selling the said lottery policy, as deponent is informed and verily believes, a peace officer, or special policeman for the County of Kings. Deponent was present when the said Phillips was arrested and saw the said manifold-book with said lottery policy recorded on the same, and also a special policeman's badge, both seized in the possession of said Phillips.

Deponent further says, that he is informed and believes that the records of the court will show, prior to 1881, that Andrew McClellan was convicted and sentenced to imprisonment for a prior offence of selling what are commonly called lottery policies. That that fact was known to the said Isaac S. Catlin, and, further, that the said Andrew McClellan did conduct an extensive business, in the city of Brooklyn, in lottery policies after being released from the term of imprisonment as aforesaid. And the evidence against the said McClellan will be the testimony of an eye-witness, who saw him write and sell the said lottery policy, upon which he was arrested, charged with selling, in 1881 ; and deponent is informed and verily believes that there is full and ample evidence to convict the said Andrew McClellan if the case had been properly tried.

Deponent further says, that notwithstanding the large number of arrests made in 1881, none of the said cases were prosecuted to conviction by the said Isaac S. Catlin until Feb., 1882 ; that on or about the 5th day of Feb., 1882, William Stone was tried and convicted in the Sessions Court, and after conviction was allowed to go on bail ; that sentence was not moved for, in said case, by the District Attorney until December, 1882.

That on or about the 7th day of June, 1882, John Mangin, John L. Walker and Charles W. Smith were all convicted in the City Court, but neither of them have been sentenced as yet. That on or about the 12th day of June Carl Fuller was convicted in the City Court of Brooklyn, and that all of these men after conviction were allowed to go on bail, and that the said District Attorney has utterly omitted and failed to bring the said cases before the court for sentence. And further, that, notwithstanding the fact that Carl Fuller had been frequently arrested for selling lottery policies, and that both prior to the date of his conviction and afterwards he had continued the business and been arrested for the same. And further, that on the 5th day of December, 1883, the said Fuller was arrested and held for examination charged with further selling lottery policies. That on the 31st day of December, 1883, notwithstanding these facts, all of the cases which the said Isaac S. Catlin had omitted and failed to prosecute were dismissed on motion of the District Attorney, and the said Isaac S. Catlin did utterly and unlawfully omit to prosecute the said Fuller.

Wherefore deponent prays, that the Grand Jury in and for the County of Kings be directed by the Court to inquire into the facts, and if the said Isaac S. Catlin omitted to prosecute any or all of the above defendants, and if he, the said Catlin, failed to discharge the duty imposed upon him by Section 349 of the Penal Code, and by his oath of office as District Attorney for the County of Kings, that he may be apprehended and dealt with according to law.

Subscribed and sworn to before me this ⎱
—— day of February, 1884.   ⎰ ANTHONY COMSTOCK.

DID MR. RIDGWAY HAVE "REASON TO BELIEVE"?

Besides the above, a letter was sent detailing some of the then pending cases, giving names of criminals and the witnesses against them.

LETTER TO MR. RIDGWAY, MARCH 10, 1884.

NEW YORK, *March* 10, 1884.

Hon. JAMES W. RIDGWAY,
        District Attorney, County of Kings,
            Brooklyn, N. Y.

Dear Sir:—

I would respectfully call your attention to the following persons who were arrested and indicted for selling policy and lottery tickets in the City of Brooklyn, and who were not prosecuted by the former District Attorney, but indictments against whom were dismissed on the last day of the term. These cases, in each instance the evidence is positive of their guilt, as I believe, and I have a full knowledge of the facts, to wit: .

The People *vs.* Maurice Foster, and Andrew D. Phillips. Witnesses, R. A. Verplank and Anthony Comstock.

The evidence consists of the policies sold to Verplank by the defendants, and the manifold-book containing the records of the plays which were seized by myself at the time of the arrest. The date of the offence was June 2, 1883, and June 22, 1883. The papers are filed in your office in each case.

Elizabeth Kepple, George E. Oram and Detective Druhan, of the Eighth Precinct, witnesses.

ABRAHAM DELA MOTTA.   GEORGE E. ORAM.
HENRY DELA MOTTA.   Witness.

In these last two cases there is an indictment now pending, upon which I believe neither of the defendants has ever been called upon to plead. They are old offenders, and I appeal to you to have them brought up and prosecuted forthwith.

The People *vs.* Andrew McClellan. George E. Oram, witness.

This man is an old offender, as you perhaps know from general rumor, and I appeal to you that he may not go unwhipped of justice. He was convicted before General Catlin's day and has escaped conviction now simply because the District Attorney failed to do his duty. We have the papers which McClellan wrote himself.

The People *vs.* Charles Stange and William Steiner. George E. Oram, witness.

The People *vs.* James G. Roe. George E. Oram, witness.

The People *vs.* Simeon Cryer. George E. Oram, witness.

The People *vs.* Thomas Ricker. George E. Oram, witness.

The People *vs.* Peter Vanderhorf and Catherine Vanderhorf. George E. Oram and Detective Druhan, witnesses.

In each of the above cases there is full and ample evidence to establish the guilt, and the only reason that these parties have not been convicted, so far as I am able to judge, is the fact that Isaac S. Catlin, as District Attorney, failed to discharge his duty as District Attorney and violated the Penal Code by such neglect.

In each of these cases I think there is full and ample evidence to convict, and in some of them the parties have been arrested more than once, and I believe are still carrying on the business. You will find the exhibits in each of these cases attached to the complaints and papers in the office.

I would respectfully ask that, at as early a date as is convenient with the other duties of your office, these papers may be examined and the matter taken before the Grand Jury and these parties reindicted and prosecuted. Should the original papers be destroyed, I can furnish an exact copy of the same in each case, as I made a copy personally and kept the same when the original complaints were made out.

Very truly yours,

ANTHONY COMSTOCK,

Secretary.

His attention was also called especially to the untried indictments against the pool gamblers and policemen who had been arrested in September, 1883, on the complaints of the agents of this Society. Their names are as follows :

POLICEMEN.

John Y. McKane, Chief of Police.
John Finnigan,   Policeman.

John Dunply,	Policeman.
Arnold Gruber,	do.
Garretson Morris,	do.
Edward Fagan,	do.
Richard Fortune,	do.
Wm. Boyle,	**do.**

POOL GAMBLERS.

Charles Smith.

Michael J. Kelly, alias Tully.

James E. Brown.

Thomas Wilson.

. Albert Burtis.

Louis Leader.

James Martin.

Jane A. Madigan and James F. Quigley, the latter also one of McKane's subordinate policemen, were also indicted and arrested for running a faro gambling game.

NOT ONE EVER TRIED.

It will be of more than passing importance to note the fact that *not one of these indictments has been tried down to the present time.*

NO WITNESSES EVER CALLED.

Notwithstanding all of the statements made by Mr. Ridgway to the contrary, one fact remains which is worthy of especial moment.

Not a witness has been called into court or before any Grand Jury to testify in a single one of the cases of common gamblers named in the foregoing affidavit, or letter of March 10, 1884; nor against Isaac S. Catlin, for violating Section 349, Penal Code; nor against the pool gamblers or John Y. McKane or any of his eight subordinates who were indicted September, 1883; nor against either of the Dela Mottas. The first indictments against the Dela Mottas were dismissed while those for second offences were pending. Upon the latter indictments neither defendant has yet been arraigned to plead.

We furnished Mr. Ridgway the names of the offenders, the crime of which they had been guilty, and the names of the witnesses to prove those crimes.

He says the Grand Jury passed upon the cases and refused to indict.

How could the Grand Jury pass upon them without any evidence? It was Mr. Ridgway's duty to have subpœnaed the witnesses before the Grand Jury. This he had the power to do at any time they were in session. This he never has done, nor has a witness thus far been called into court by him on one of the foregoing cases.

This may be said to be ancient history. It might well be so considered, did not the fact that it was brought into the administration of Mr. Ridgway revive it, and place the responsibility anew upon the present occupant of the office of District Attorney of Kings County.

Just here it will be interesting to note the testimony of five different persons concerning the dismissal of these indictments.

It will lend interest to the reader to remember that all of these gentlemen were under oath.

At a session of the Bacon Legislative Investigating Committee Mr. Ridgway first gave his version concerning these cases.

On page 684, Printed Report, appears the following:

Q. Mr. Ridgway, did you ever investigate the circumstances under which that large number of indictments were *nolle prossed* in the month of December, 1883?

A. Yes, sir; I was about to investigate the matter. Soon after my attention was called to it, I went to General Catlin and asked him about it. He said they had been dismissed on motion before the Court. He informed me that the parties had gone out of business and were no longer breaking the law. He dismissed them.

Q. When did this conversation take place?

A. It was some time afterward, when my attention was called to it.

Foster L. Backus, an assistant of Mr. Catlin, being sworn before the Investigating Committee, testifies to the evidence to support these indictments as follows:

" I told General Catlin in Mr. Bacon's (Catlin's chief clerk) presence that every case that I had tried where Mr. Comstock furnished the evidence, or where his men were the witnesses, we had obtained a conviction, and that the evidence was substantially the same in the other cases."   *   *   *

John Oakey, another of Mr. Catlin's assistants (p. 935), swears as follows:

" I was in the Court of Sessions trying cases, and Mr. Bacon came in with this large bundle of indictments, a very great many of them; I made the motion to Judge Moore to *nolle* these indictments. I took up perhaps a half dozen and told him the reason why: that the complaining witnesses were dead; those that were *nolled* on account of the witnesses not being able to be found; several cases were *nolled* on account of the death of the defendant. Having read a number of them, I said to Judge Moore that was the general nature of these indictments and moved to *nolle* them, and they were handed to Mr. York and that was all that was ever done about it; and after that there came into the office one or two scattering indictments, some that were overlooked or something of that kind, and they found out the reason why, and they were *nolled;* a very few, not over three or four, perhaps."

Mr. Catlin, in explaining how these indictments came to be dismissed, testified under oath before the Investigating Committee as follows:

Q. Have you ever heard any satisfactory explanation of that occurrence?

A. No, sir; I have heard speculation on the subject.

Q. From whom?

A. From Colonel Oakey and Mr. Backus, and those that I have made myself: that there were large piles of indictments, and that these indictments might, by mistake, have gotten into those piles in the hurry to transfer the books, papers, and documents over to Mr. Ridgway; in other words, they were together; that is, in the immediate vicinity of each other, and they might have been, by mistake, placed into the piles that were dismissed.   I can only make that explanation, or else charge absolute malcfeasance upon some one, and which one I do not know.

Bernard J. York, clerk of the Court of Sessions, being sworn, says, in reference to these same cases :

"Nine were dismissed on December 22, five December 26, eighteen December 29, and twenty-five December 31."

He then goes on and states as to the total number of indictments dismissed on certain dates as follows :

"On the 26th day of December the number dismissed was nine.   That includes five that I testified to before as gambling indictments, making four other than those of gambling.

"December 29, twenty-two dismissed, in all, including eighteen gambling indictments, making four that were not gambling.

"December 31, thirty-seven indictments dismissed, including twenty-five designated heretofore as gambling."

This record, produced from the minutes of the Court, plays sad havoc with the sworn statements of Messrs. Oakey and Catlin.

Unfortunately for Mr. Catlin there was not a very large amount of indictments dismissed on either the 26th, 29th or the 31st days of December, when the major portion of these fifty-seven indictments were dismissed, if Mr. York's minutes are correct.   I leave the reader to surmise, how, on the 26th of December, the five gambling indictments that were dismissed could have mysteriously got mixed up with "the large pile " of four others so as to deceive the one who had charge of the dismissal of these indictments; or how, on the 29th of December, the eighteen gambling indictments could have got mixed up with "the large pile" of four other indictments dismissed on that day; or how the twenty-five gambling indictments on December 31st could have got mixed up with "the large pile " of twelve other indictments dismissed upon that day.

There is, however, another theory, that can be very briefly stated and to my mind is a better explanation of this matter than any that has been given.

December 20, Mr. Backus was trying cases in the Sessions Court in Brooklyn. He sent a messenger over to my office, summoning the writer to appear at once in his court, without specifying any cases that were up for trial. As the writer was engaged in Court (having come from the General Sessions Court in New York City, where a case had been disposed of, and was on his way to the United States Court, where a case was pending before United States Commissioner Shields) when he received the message, the following letter was sent to Mr. Backus, which will fully explain the writer's position and the reason why he did not respond to the invitation of Mr. Backus's messenger.

December, 20, 1883.

Mr. BACKUS,
    Assistant District Attorney,
        Brooklyn, N. Y.

Dear Sir :—

Upon my return, a few moments ago, to this office I was informed by my assistant that a messenger was here asking me to come to Brooklyn at once, that you desired to see me.

I should be only too glad to comply with your request, only that I am just going to the United States Court in a case there before one of the Commissioners, which may occupy the balance of the afternoon. I have matters in the State Court which I must go and attend to, and other duties which have piled up on account of my being two days in the Oyer and Terminer Court this week and yesterday absent in Goshen trying a case there.

In order that you may see exactly how pressed I am for this week, and indeed for the balance of the year, I beg just to call your attention to my situation.

On the 21st, to-morrow, I have three cases for trial in Special Sessions Court, which have been adjourned over from this week in order to enable me to be present in the Oyer and Terminer Court.

Saturday I have three more cases in the Tombs Police Court at 10:30 A.M.

Monday we have three cases in Brooklyn at 1:30 P.M., set peremptorily for examination.

Tuesday is Christmas.

Wednesday we have two cases set for trial in Special Sessions Court, for which we are summoned.

Then there are cases to come up on the other days, so that for the balance of the year we have cases in the courts ; and if you can tell me, my good friend, how I can possibly be in two places at one time, I shall be only too glad to respond.

Now will it not do for me to see you on Monday, when we come over to Brooklyn in the Fuller case?

If I can get through this afternoon so as to get time to come over and see you, I will endeavor to do so. You can send word by the messenger if you desire to have me call this afternoon.

Very truly yours,
(signed) ANTHONY COMSTOCK,
Secretary,
Per D.

No message came, and he did not see me the following Monday, although the case of the notorious Carl Fuller was before Justice Walsh, in Brooklyn, for examination on his sixth offence and arrest.

This letter was mailed on the 20th and doubtless received on the 21st.

Now, let this fact be noted : that throughout all these years these gamblers had been protected from prosecution, despite our earnest protests and appeals that they be brought to justice ; and even the four who had been convicted in June, 1882, had never been sentenced. Fuller was one of these four.

The next day, after the District Attorney's office became informed of the fact that we could not be there, they began to dismiss the fifty-seven indictments that had not been prosecuted, and kept up the dismissal of those indictments until the 31st, when they dismissed the last twenty-five. The record of the Court, sworn to by Mr. York, confirms this statement.

If the two Dela Mottas were not protected absolutely,

why were the first two indictments dismissed for the first
offence and they never called upon to plead to the second
indictment at all during Mr. Catlin's administration ?

Andy McClellan was a boss gambler who had been previously convicted. Mr. Catlin himself swears he knew
McClellan had been convicted for policy gambling before he
(Catlin) went into office. General Catlin in May, 1881,
was especially solicitous that I should get the evidence
against him, in order that he might prosecute him. Yet,
after securing the evidence against him and his right bower,
Charles W. Smith, the most that we could accomplish from
May, 1881, throughout Mr. Catlin's administration, was to secure the conviction of Smith in the City Court, in June, 1882, on
one indictment, while three other indictments against him,
and all of the indictments against Andy McClellan, were
dismissed in December, 1883, and that, too, in face of the
fact that this business continued right on in the city of
Brooklyn.

Charles W. Smith, McClellan's right-hand man, was *never
sentenced during Catlin's administration.* What more could
the administration of the District Attorney's office do for
Andy McClellan and Charles W. Smith, and the other gamblers who turned their policy books into Andy McClellan's
headquarters, than they did during the years 1881, 1882, and
1883 by protecting them from prosecution on the indictments
found against them through the efforts of the Society for the
Suppression of Vice, and then during the last ten days of
that administration DISMISS all of these indictments against
these common gamblers ? and that, too, notwithstanding that
their crime was a FELONY, and the evidence of their guilt, as
Mr. Backus testified, was absolute.

Does the testimony of the gentleman aforesaid help Mr.
Ridgway's cause in the matter of his failure to prosecute
these common gamblers ?

Were not these common gamblers thoroughly and completely protected by the Catlin administration, whether General Catlin intended it or not? What of the urgent appeals made by our Society for the vigorous prosecution of these men which Mr. Catlin and his assistants disregarded?

DID MR. RIDGWAY KNOW?

Knowledge is an element of guilt.

As has been seen, Section 349 of the Penal Code makes it the duty of District Attorneys, Sheriffs, etc., "to inform against and prosecute all persons whom they have *reason to believe* offenders against the provisions" of Chapter IX. of the Penal Code, which includes gambling of all descriptions.

The testimony of an eye-witness is always valuable; when supported by documentary evidence it is still more so. Let us, therefore, call, as the first witness to prove that the present District Attorney had "cause to believe" that the laws were being violated, Mr. James W. Ridgway and his own documents.

I present first a letter written by Mr. Ridgway, printed in the Brooklyn *Union*, April 22, 1884, to John Y. McKane, Chief of Police.

This letter was written at a time when there was no horse racing and consequently no pool-selling on either course at Coney Island. It was doubtless inspired by the fact that the Roosevelt Legislative Investigating Committee, then in session, were making it exceedingly lively for gamblers in New York County. This letter, as soon as written, was given to the press, as it was published the same afternoon, as follows:

OFFICE OF THE DISTRICT ATTORNEY,
BROOKLYN, *April* 22, 1884.

JOHN Y. McKANE, Esq.,
Chief of Police, Town of Gravesend.

Dear Sir:—I desire to call your attention to the fact that it is a matter of public notoriety that gambling is openly carried on at various places at Coney Island, in the township over which you hold police supervision.

It is hardly necessary for me to call your attention to the fact that gambling is prohibited by the laws of our State, and to remind you of the obligation you owe to the people, by virtue of your office, to enforce the laws. The particular place alluded to is one resorted to by thousands of the people of our city, to whom such exhibition is objectionable.

The season is now about opening, and active measures should be at once taken to make Coney Island free from all such practices as tend to make it repulsive to decent people.

Very respectfully yours,
JAMES W. RIDGWAY,
District Attorney.

In connection with this letter appeared in the same paper an interview with Mr. Ridgway, which has a very significant bearing upon his knowledge and duty. He says :

"I would like to add in this connection that there was a bill before the Legislature to permit pool-selling on the race tracks, and the law-makers of this State do not seem to have found anything to justify them in passing such a law. THEY HAVE THEREFORE THROWN THE WHOLE RESPONSIBILITY UPON THE OFFICE OF THE DISTRICT ATTORNEY, AND IF HE DOES NOT DO HIS DUTY HE SHOULD BE REMOVED from office. If the people admit that pool-selling is a harmless amusement, their representatives in the Legislature should legalize it.

"So long as the law against pool-selling remains upon the statute books, and I am in office, I will do what I can to have it enforced."

Has he done all he could have done ? In the light of the record of these gambling cases, with the condensed rays of the historic reflector turned back upon these fair-sounding words, I ask the candid reader, after he shall have read the facts, to say whether or no these words were not as hollow as sounding brass, and if the manifest intent was not to bring the gamblers to terms, not to justice ?

May 27 there were published in most of the New York morning papers interviews purporting to come from Mr. Ridgway, all of the same purport. The New York *Sun*, May 27, 1884, says :

4

" District Attorney Ridgway of Kings County said yesterday in reference to pool-selling on Coney Island : ' I am going to institute criminal
proceedings at once against every man engaged in pool-selling, and if I
don't break it up it will be because the machinery of the law is not
strong enough to do it.   I notified the Brighton Beach track people that
they must not sell pools nor allow other gambling.   I had men there to
watch them on Saturday.   I am aware they did not heed my warning, and
I shall take the case of every man interested in gambling of any kind
before the Grand Jury.'"

June 3, 1884, the week following Mr. Ridgway's proclamation, Judge Moore, in charging the Grand Jury of Kings
County Court of Sessions, is reported in various papers as
saying, concerning pool-selling at Coney Island :

" The violation of law," he said, " in the town of Gravesend was persistent, flagrant, and open.   The law made pool-selling a crime, and it
was the duty of the District Attorney to cause the arrest of persons
engaged in it."

In face of Mr. Ridgway's proclamation and Judge Moore's
charge to the Grand Jury, not a single one of the Brighton
Beach gamblers, whom Mr. Ridgway had " men to watch,"
and of whom he said, " I am aware they did not heed my
warning," were indicted ; and we challenge him to show by
the records of that Grand Jury a single *name of any gambler
that he ever brought before that Grand Jury.*

Early in June a Gravesend official came to our office and
politely informed me that it was worth $5000 to me if I
would not interfere with the Coney Island Jockey Club
gamblers.   Encouraged by the words of Judge Moore and
Mr. Ridgway, we thought that we would now have hearty
co-operation, and in order to resent the insult of a bribe and
to assist what we believed was an earnest determination to
enforce the law on their part, we sent men down to the Coney
Island Jockey Club race course, June 16, 1884, and secured
the evidence against a number of gamblers who were then
and there *openly* violating the law.   We did not send men

to Brighton Beach, as Mr. Ridgway had announced to the gamblers as well as to the public that he "had men watching them."

We did not intend or desire to interfere with Mr. Ridgway's plans. Affidavits were prepared against the gamblers by our men, and on the following day (June 17) were taken to the District Attorney's office. We found Mr. Ridgway absent from the city, and Mr. Shorter, first assistant District Attorney, in charge of the office. The facts were presented to Mr. Shorter, and he was asked to go before one of the County or Supreme Court Judges, secure warrants and search warrants, and have these men arrested and their unlawful paraphernalia seized. Mr. Shorter was informed that the laws were being openly violated by professional gamblers. He was further informed of the rumors that were then in vogue wherein it was charged that the gamblers had made a contract and that an agreement had been made on the part of the District Attorney that they should not be interfered with.

I desire to emphasize, just here, that *we did not believe these rumors at that time.* We laid them before the prosecuting attorney and his assistants as *reasons why* vigorous action should be taken at once ; for not only were the laws being violated, but the character and standing of officials were scandalized by these rumors. It was charged at the time that the gamblers had "fixed every one ; even Comstock had been fixed and would do nothing."

It is a rule of our office, whenever we hear of any gamblers or other criminals claiming that they have "fixed" our office, or that they have made any agreement or contract by which they can continue to violate the law, to immediately secure the evidence against, and forthwith arrest and bring them into court, put our agents upon the witness-stand where the defendants or their counsel have the fullest latitude for cross-examination, and then challenge them to prove their libel against us under these, to them, most favorable circumstances.

Being obliged to wait until the 23d, when we were advised Mr. Ridgway would return, June 21 we again sent our men down to this same place, who secured additional evidence against the same men whom they had found violating the law on the 16th, and also against others, making twenty-two gamblers altogether against whom we had secured positive evidence. Affidavits, warrants, and search warrants were drawn, and these papers were taken June 23, 1884, personally to Mr. Ridgway by Mr. W. C. Beecher, counsel for this Society, and the writer.

CHAPTER V.

WHAT MR. RIDGWAY SAID AND DID.

MONDAY, June 23, 1884, Mr. W. C. Beecher and myself called upon Mr. Ridgway, directed his attention to the flagrant and open violations of law at Sheepshead Bay race course, and informed him that we had the evidence against twenty-two different gamblers, presented complaints drawn in affidavit form against these parties, and asked for warrants and search warrants to arrest the gamblers and seize their unlawful paraphernalia. Mr. Ridgway advised against warrants before a magistrate, but said he would personally take the cases before the Grand Jury on the 25th of June. He was then informed that it was rumored and charged that the gamblers were boasting that nothing would be done to them ; that it was claimed that James E. Kelly had paid or agreed to pay $50,000 upon an agreement and contract that he and his associate gamblers were not to be interfered with ; that it was charged by these rumors that J. E. Kelly had had a private interview with him, and that the District Attorney had agreed that no interference would be permitted with those on the Coney Island Jockey Club race course throughout the season.

Mr. Ridgway replied with an oath that he " would like very much to fix it definitely upon some man, and he would show him," but made no further denial. We told him that we had seen his interview in the *Union*, and were glad to be able to furnish him evidence upon which these men could be arrested and convicted. We believed him sincere, and went away satisfied with his promise to take the matter before the Grand Jury in person on the 25th.

June 25, 1884, at ten o'clock we were in Brooklyn with the witnesses in these cases in the waiting-room of the Grand Jury. The affidavits were all drawn and exhibits attached giving the full facts in writing, in affidavit form, which were again that morning submitted to Mr. Ridgway. Mr. Ridgway then informed us that Mr. Shorter, his first assistant, had charge of the Grand Jury, and directed us to go up to the Grand Jury rooms, as the matter was to come up that morning. Messrs. Britton, Oram, Baldwin, and myself—witnesses —reported to Mr. Shorter, showing him the papers and evidence in the different cases. He saw and talked with the witnesses, who were all present. We were kept waiting until after one o'clock, when Mr. Shorter informed us that our cases would not be taken up that day. We then went down and had another interview with Mr. Ridgway. He was told that fresh rumors had reached our office "that gamblers at Sheepshead Bay race track were not to be raided or anything done to them until after the races closed the next week." The complaints were then again presented to him. These complaints set out in detail the facts against each gambler, and also established the fact that eye-witnesses had seen the paraphernalia used for registering bets and wagers, and that from fifty to one hundred persons were engaged in violating the law at this course. He was asked that, inasmuch as the Grand Jury had not acted, he take the matters forthwith before Judge Moore for warrants and search warrants.

We urged that, because of the rumors, it was a case where we ought to go before one of the higher judges and have warrants and search warrants issued at once and make these men feel something of the rigor of the law. Mr. Ridgway declined, saying he " thought the best thing to be done was to let the Grand Jury act ; that if we went before

Judge Moore for a warrant, he would not try the cases or permit them to go before his Grand Jury, and that would throw them into the Oyer and Terminer Court, which had no Grand Jury until next fall."

We presented that these gamblers were openly violating the law at Sheepshead Bay, and that it was important to make an example of them ; and that the best way to nail the lies against him and other officials was, now that we had the evidence against these men, to arrest them and seize their unlawful matter. We urged with much earnestness that, inasmuch as these rumors of contracts were made against his office, the way to vindicate himself and nail these lies was to raid the men, as we had raided them in other places.

It was conceded that the justices of Gravesend were not the proper persons to apply to for warrants in these cases, inasmuch as their subordinates were aiding and assisting gamblers. The justices had it in their power to summon these policemen before them as witnesses against the gamblers if they had been so disposed, but did not. As police commissioners they could have ordered them to suppress gambling, which they did not do.

At this time we discussed the action of the local magistrates at Gravesend, who being also police commissioners, had appointed their subordinates to protect and assist these gamblers in violating the law.

He assured us that the matter would come before the Grand Jury the next day, and that he would have the bills drawn immediately and filed the next morning, and bench warrants and search warrants issued as soon as the bills were filed.

On this date Mr. Ridgway admitted to Mr. Britton that he had been to the New York office of the Coney Island Jockey Club personally and given them notice that he should proceed against them if they violated the law. He also admitted the same thing to the writer.

Thursday, June 26, at ten o'clock we again presented ourselves as witnesses for the Grand Jury. Messrs. Oram, Britton, Baldwin, and myself were called and examined in one case. After a little, Mr. Shorter came out of the Grand Jury room and informed us that we need not wait, as there would not be any more of our cases taken up that day. A protest was made against delay; but Mr. Shorter said "it made no difference." We then went in search of Mr. Ridgway; he was nowhere to be found. We then looked for Judge Pratt, and found that he was in Massachusetts. We then went in search of Judge Brown, but found that he was in Newburg, while Judge Bartlett was actually holding court and we could not see him. We then went to Judge Moore's court, but found that he had adjourned court and gone away; then up to Judge Moore's house, taking the witnesses, complaints, and exhibits with us. When we inquired for him and sent in our names, we were informed that he was too ill to be seen. Determined not to be thwarted, and bound to do all in our power to enforce the laws so brazenly violated, we then went back to the court-house, and about two o'clock went up to the ante-room of the Grand Jury and found the Grand Jury about to adjourn. In the presence of Mr. Oram and others a demand was made upon Mr. Shorter, as follows :—" Mr. Shorter, in the presence of witnesses I now demand of you that these matters be taken before the Grand Jury forthwith before they adjourn; that unless you take the matter up forthwith, I will go directly to the Governor of the State." Mr. Shorter said he did not propose to take the odium or responsibility, that he would present the matter to the Grand Jury.

As a result, *the balance of our twenty-two cases were promptly called before the Grand Jury and within an hour indictments found.* A tender to Mr. Shorter was made of the services, without charge, of the stenographer and agents of our Society to do the clerical work in the preparation of these indictments, so as to have the indictments promptly gotten out. He was also told that Mr. Ridgway had promised to have the indictments prepared immediately, so that they could be presented to the Court as soon as the Grand Jury should order them. The same offer was made to the chief clerk. They informed us that it would not be necessary; that they could easily prepare them themselves, and have them ready in time the next morning.

The next morning the Grand Jury came together, but as there were no bills of indictments ready for them to sign, they were obliged to adjourn until Monday, giving the gamblers Friday and Saturday to violate the law without molestation.

The next day we had an interview with Judge Moore. He was informed of these cases, and of the delays, and that we had called at his house for the purpose of asking of him warrants to raid these gamblers.

To our great surprise, we were treated in a most abrupt manner. It was made to appear that we had done something out of the proper and ordinary course of procedure ; and we were further informed, in most emphatic terms, that he would not issue a warrant. He informed us that he would consider nothing unless it came through the District Attorney. We respectfully submitted that it was our right, as citizens, under the Code to apply to any magistrate for assistance in enforcing the law. We were rebuked for our pains.

That the reader may not think us over-presumptuous, and at the same time be advised of the provisions of law, and the powers and duties of a magistrate, we present the following. We ask careful attention to these provisions of the Code of Criminal Procedure. Is it the duty of a magistrate to prevent crime and enforce the law when the facts are brought to his attention ?

MAGISTRATE DEFINED.

The Code of Criminal Procedure defines a magistrate as follows :—

"Section 146. A magistrate is an officer having power to issue a warrant for the arrest of a person charged with a crime."

The next section designates "who are magistrates" as follows :—

"Section 147. The following persons are magistrates:
1. The judges of the Supreme Court;
2. The judges of any City Court;
3. The *County judges* and *special County judges*," etc.

POWER AND DUTY OF MAGISTRATE.

The next section defines the duty of a magistrate, as follows :

"Section 148. When an information is laid before a magistrate of the commission of a crime, *he must examine* on oath the informant and prosecutor, and any other witnesses he may produce, and take their depositions in writing, and cause them to be subscribed by the parties making them."

It will be observed that this section does not say "may," but "*must examine.*"

Equally positive is Section 150, which provides as follows:

"Section 150. If the magistrate be satisfied therefrom that the crime complained of has been committed, and that there is reasonable ground to believe that the defendant has committed it, he *must* issue a warrant of arrest."

The matter of an examination is entirely another thing. For if a magistrate from any cause cannot hold an examination, the prisoners can be taken before the nearest and most accessible magistrate.

So in like manner in reference to the issuing of a search warrant. The Code of Criminal Procedure provides as follows, making it the imperative duty of the magistrate to issue a search warrant, to wit:

" Section 796. If the magistrate be thereupon satisfied of the existence of the grounds of the application, or that there is probable cause to believe their existence, *he must issue a search warrant,* signed by him with his name of office, to a peace officer in his county, commanding him *forthwith* to search the person or place named for the property specified, and bring it before the magistrate."

We stood upon our rights as citizens, and, after having secured the positive evidence of guilt, simply demanded that the criminals be brought to justice.

A magistrate is simply a servant of the people, sworn to discharge certain offices of duty, under the prescribed rules of law. No magistrate is so high that a citizen, however lowly, may not approach him and ask of him a warrant to arrest a criminal; and we submit that when a citizen does that in good faith, he is not to be denounced nor treated with contempt. We had every reason to believe that this magistrate, because of his earnest utterances from the bench, would be interested in enforcing these laws, and therefore we thought it not improper to present the facts to him and ask for a warrant.

How easy it is to be misunderstood! How different was our treatment in these cases from that in the cases of the gamblers in Long Island City! When we went to Mr. Justice Gilbert, then of the Supreme Court of the State, he not only at once received the papers, but with equal alacrity issued his warrants, and assisted us in every way, so that in one afternoon we effectually closed the four notorious gambling saloons in Long Island City. The Recorder and Judges of the General Sessions Court in New York City have frequently issued their warrants in similar cases, so that we not only felt that we had the right to ask for this assistance, but we were encouraged to expect it from the earnest words proceeding from the Court when he charged the Grand Jury concerning these very crimes. Was it not our *right* as a *citizen* to go directly to any magistrate with our complaints? Instead of rebuffing and rebuking us, is it not the imperative duty of any magistrate to at least examine the witnesses under the provisions of the Code of Criminal Procedure?

If he found the complaint well founded, "he must issue his warrant;" so says the Code.

We concede that ordinarily a magistrate of a Court of Record is not to be troubled with the detail of an arrest or preliminary examination.

There are, however, extraordinary occasions which call for heroic treatment. The fact that about 150 gamblers were openly defying the law in the face of the public proclamations of the District Attorney, and the charge of the Court to the then existing Grand Jury, seemed important enough to justify our course, especially as the local justices were Police Commissioners, whose subordinates were aiding these criminal offences, and against whom neither the Commissioners nor their policemen would move. This Court could direct the Sheriff to proceed, and had power to enforce its mandates.

Under the circumstances, was it not eminently proper that an application should be made to this Court?

June 27 another interview was had with Mr. Ridgway, wherein he was reminded that he had promised that if indictments were ordered by the Grand Jury, he would have them drawn so as to file "the next day after the bills were ordered." The matter then had gone over till Monday. He was informed that there would be a race the following day, and that the law was being and would be again "openly violated; that the races would close on Tuesday following, the first day of July; that while the races continued it would not be difficult to capture these men and their paraphernalia. After the races closed it would be very difficult to find some of the men wanted." While talking, Mr. Britton came in

and said that he had had an interview with one of the Grand
Jurors, who informed him that "they had adjourned yesterday till this morning in order to give the District Attorney
an opportunity to prepare and present the bills to them ;
that when they called for the bills they were informed they
were not ready." We again appealed for warrants, but appealed in vain.

Saturday, June 28, the gamblers were engaged in openly
violating the law. A report was brought to our office on that
day that "the Coney Island gamblers were to be notified to
appear at Mr. Ridgway's office on Monday morning and give
bail, so that their business would not be interfered with down
on the track during the races."

Monday, June 30, the Grand Jury had these twenty-two
indictments to examine, sign, and present in Court, besides
other matters ; and yet the Grand Jury had completed their
labors, filed their indictments in court, and nine of the
twenty-two gamblers, who had evidently been notified beforehand, had been to the District Attorney's office, given their
bail, and gone away—all before half-past eleven A. M.

Of those who were thus notified and voluntarily gave bail
are the following, to wit : Michael Murray, John T. Mc-
Dougall, indicted as "Dougal McDougall," James E. Kelly
Thomas Murray, John S. Stow, Mark Jordan, James Dunn,
David J. Johnson, Albert H. Cridge.

UNUSUAL ZEAL.

In the zeal to oblige the gamblers two men who were *not*
indicted, giving the names of John Kelly and Frank Snyder,
were allowed to give bail upon these indictments, Frank
Snyder being accepted in the place of Herman Schneider.
Neither of these two men had been indicted. In the "in-
decent haste" and zeal to serve the gambling fraternity, no
opportunity was given the witnesses to identify the men before they gave bail.

TEST OF MR. RIDGWAY'S SINCERITY.

As testing the sincerity of Mr. Ridgway's public utterances, made but a few days before, as already quoted, what occurred on this date, June 30, 1884? Mr. Ridgway could not be found at his office. After a long search we discovered him in the Club House in Pierrepont Street. He was asked "if bench warrants had been issued for the arrest of the other indicted gamblers?" He replied that "one of his officers had them, but that all of these men would come if they were notified." He was told : "Mr. Ridgway, these men are openly violating the law to-day, and the Code makes it the duty of the officers charged with the arrest of any of these men to seize the paraphernalia. You have the affida- vits which have been prepared, and which are now in your office, showing sufficient grounds for search warrants to be issued." He informed us that "there would be no search warrants issued; that after an indictment had been found search warrants could not be issued." To this we replied : "Mr. Ridgway, that is perfectly ridiculous. You are evi- dently not acquainted with the Code, for Section 345 makes it the *duty* of the officer authorized to arrest any of these men to *seize* this matter, and the fact that the criminal has been indicted and still continues to violate the law is a reason why he should be arrested and the matters seized, in order that the law may be felt by those who are violating it." Mr. Britton, my assistant, was present during this conversa- tion.

It was then urged upon Mr. Ridgway as a reason why these men should be arrested in due form of law, and their gambling paraphernalia seized, as follows : "Mr. Ridgway, it is charged that part of the contract is that these men are not to be arrested nor interfered with on the race track." Mr. Ridgway replied, with an oath, he didn't care a ——

—— what people said; that he proposed to send an officer down there to notify these men, even if it was necessary to send all of the 54 men, or men from the 54 booths, up to his office to be identified; that Kelly had been to him and told him that he would send all of the men up. He then said: " I understand you have been talking about my office." The writer replied in substance and effect as follows: "The most said was that I thought it was very strange that every one of the principal gamblers of the Sheepshead Bay race-track should be on hand in your office ready to give bail before the indictments were filed, and that bail-bonds in all these cases could be prepared, signed, and executed before 11:30 A. M., when the indictments were not filed in court until after half-past ten o'clock. Certain it is that your officers have not had time to go and look up these gamblers and bring them over here after the indictments were filed. Some of the men could not be identified unless our men identified them. Our men are here now to identify these men." A demand was also made that, under the affidavits then in his office, he apply for search warrants to seize the gamblers' unlawful matter. He said it would not be done. That if we would send one of our officers down with his men to identify the persons who had been indicted, his officer would notify them that they had been indicted, and that they (the gamblers) would appear the next day and give bail.

In this connection note Section 156 of the Penal Code, which makes it a misdemeanor to disclose to an indicted person before his arrest the fact that he has been indicted.

" Sec. 156.—A judge, grand juror, district attorney, clerk, or other officer who, except in the due discharge of his official duty, discloses before an accused person is in custody the fact of an indictment having been ordered against him is guilty of a misdemeanor."

After we found that Mr. Ridgway was determined to protect and shield these men from arrest in face of the rumors

of a contract made to the effect that "the gamblers should
not be arrested nor their paraphernalia or unlawful business
interfered with," and prostitute the ends of justice in their
behalf by sending his men to notify them of the action of
the Grand Jury before they were arrested, an application
was made at the office of the Brooklyn *Union* that they should
send a trusty man with the officer and our agent and make a
faithful report of what occurred. A gentleman above reproach was sent, and here is his testimony of what occurred :

The Brooklyn *Union* of July 1, 1884, says, under the
title of

"A PUBLIC FARCE."

"Mr. James E. Kelly, of pool-selling notoriety, stood in his little box
in the betting amphitheatre at the Coney Island Jockey Club yesterday
afternoon engaged in his usual lively occupation of calling out the odds
on the races and raking in the shekels of the over-trustful. He did not
seem to be in the least disturbed by the fact that he had just been indicted for violating the law of the State and had that very morning been
obliged to find bail. Just before the third race was called a sprucely
dressed young man with an abnormally developed nose touched Mr.
Kelly on the shoulder and informed him that he was from the District
Attorney's office, and would like to speak with him privately for a few
moments, at the same time apologizing to Mr. Kelly for disturbing him
during business hours. The young man, who was of the District Attorney's office, was accompanied by Jere Wernberg, the attorney for
the pool-sellers, and by Mr. Joseph A. Britton, an agent of the Society for the Prevention of Crime. There were twenty-three indictments
found by the Grand Jury against the Sheepshead Bay pool-sellers."

What happened at the race track is further disclosed in
the same article. After stating that all of the principal persons wanted had come to the District Attorney's office and
given bail that morning, the article says :

"Mr. Comstock's agent visited the track yesterday in order to identify
the remaining twelve; the District Attorney's representative came to
serve the papers upon the accused and request them to appear before

Mr. Ridgway to-day. Of course the whole thing was nothing but a farce, and was so regarded by everybody concerned. Mr. Kelly went around with Mr. Britton and Mr. . . . . . and the following men were identified and served with notices to appear: John White, F. T. Bradley, T. J. Meehan, D. Gleason, F. Rodman, James Fry, William McNamara, William Waring, J. Varley and D. Wartzfelder."

Note the further important testimony of this impartial eye-witness, who can be corroborated if necessary. He says in the same article :

"The business of pool-selling was not for a moment interfered with, and the pool-sellers who had been indicted laughed and hob-nobbed with Mr. Jere Wernberg and the representative of the District Attorney's office."

Mr. Kelly is reported also in the same article, by the same witness, as assuring his brother gamblers that there was nothing to fear.

" You know," he said, " half of you are indicted under wrong names, and even if there was a case against you, nothing will come of it. The Grand Jury will adjourn, the case will be put off till fall, and then they will be pigeon-holed or you will be let off with a small fine, and that will end the whole matter. *At any rate, our business will not be interfered with this season.*"

Has not this prophecy of Mr. Kelly been fulfilled? Did Mr. Kelly speak with a knowledge of a contract of protection being in force? Certain it is that his very positive words would indicate that he felt confident that some power was to deliver him from the hands of the law. It will be of interest to note how this matter was "pigeon-holed" when we come further to consider these cases.

The same paper contained an interview with Mr. Ridgway in which he complacently says : " I have done my best in this thing ; I have worked hard and done my duty, and those who don't like it can do as they d——n please."

These words going to the public made it appear that he was very zealous.

5

Up to June 30, 1884, we had not believed the rumors that the gamblers were to be "protected" and that we were not to be permitted to raid them, as we had successfully done in other cases, especially after bench warrants would be issued for their arrest. We repeatedly plead these rumors of contracts for protection as arguments for prompt and vigorous action, not believing them true. The refusal to allow the gamblers to be arrested after the Grand Jury had indicted them forced us to believe that Mr. Ridgway was not acting in good faith ; and it is for the reader to say whether any man would voluntarily go out of his way to protect gamblers openly violating the law if there was not some very strong consideration presented as an inducement for thus braving public opinion, defying the obligations of office, and violating the Penal Code.

FARCE NO. II.

July 8 the parties indicted who had given bail were to be arraigned before Judge Moore in the Sessions Court. In the cases of Albert H. Cridge, James E. Kelly, Thomas Murray, John S. Stow, David J. Johnson, John T. McDougall, alias Dougal McDougall, James Dunn, Michael Murray, Mark Jordan, when called, their counsel demurred to their indictments. The other parties who had given bail on the 1st day of July, with the exception of Wartzfelder, Rose, and John Kelly, were present in court. The names under which they had been indicted, and under which they had given bail, were called, and each one of them was *permitted to remain mute in his seat*, although Mr. Jenks, the assistant District Attorney, was notified that they were present and that the witnesses were there to identify them. Yet he neither called the attention of the court to the fact that they were present, nor did he insist upon their appearing to plead, but *allowed them to walk out of court in contempt of the proceedings.*

Some of these men were, as they claimed, indicted under erroneous names. When the officer at the gambling booths informed them of their indictment he informed them also of the names under which they had been indicted.

July 1 the gamblers thus favored by Mr. Ridgway and his officers *voluntarily* came to the District Attorney's office and gave bail.

Each man gave his right name and the name under which he had been indicted. Each bail-bond contained both of these names.

One case will illustrate all. John T. McDougall was one of the bosses, and one of the favored nine who had been in waiting in the District Attorney's office, June 30, for the Grand Jury to present their indictment to the court, in order to give bail thereon. This was to prevent annoyance or interference during business hours at the gambling booths. McDougall had been known to the witnesses, and indicted, by the name of " Dougal McDougall." He was the only McDougall doing business at the Sheepshead Bay race track, so far as the witnesses knew. A certified copy of his bond, now before me, dated June 30, 1884, reads as follows:

"An indictment having been found on the 30th day of June, 1884, in the Court of Sessions of Kings County, charging Dougal McDougall, whose true name is John McDougall, with the crime of recording bets and wagers.

(Signed)   "JOHN T. McDOUGALL."

The right names, or names they claimed to be their right names, of these men were first discovered when Mr. Ridgway's officers went to the gamblers, after indictment, and found them openly violating the law, apologizing for interfering with their unlawful business, notified them of their indictments, and informed them of the name under which each had been indicted; when the gamblers, with equal courtesy, informed the peace officer, whose duty it was to

arrest, but who did not arrest these criminals, what their right
names were.

FICTITIOUS NAMES.

Some one will suppose, perhaps, that because these men
claimed they were indicted under fictitious or erroneous
names, this was a fatal defect in the indictment or a proper
excuse for the District Attorney not moving against them,
or that we were to blame for not getting their right names.

It is a very difficult thing to secure the right name of a
criminal before arrest.   It would be apt to arouse suspicion
and put a criminal upon his guard to attempt to secure his
true name, especially as so many have numerous names as
a cover to their criminal doings.

It is not necessary to have the true name.   The important thing is to get the *right person.*

The Code of Criminal Procedure clearly settles this.
Section 277 takes away all excuses from the District Attorney and remedies all defects arising from " fictitious " or
" erroneous " names.   It says :

"Section 277. If a defendant is indicted by a fictitious or erroneous
name, and in any stage of the proceedings his true name is discovered,
it may be inserted in the subsequent proceedings, referring to the
fact of his being indicted by the name mentioned in the indictment."

By their own voluntary act these men had discovered their
true names to the District Attorney, and then voluntarily
entered bail accordingly.

Our indictments were regular, our evidence positive,
and our witnesses unimpeached, and yet the facts concerning these cases will savor of some deep-laid plot to thwart
the ends of justice and screen these guilty gamblers from
merited punishment.

Will the District Attorney and his assistant plead that they
did not know the right names, as a defence for this farce ? If
so, we produce the bail-bond of these men as the first evi-

dence; and, second, the fact that in open court Mr. Jenks, the assistant District Attorney, was told that "each of the defendants was present," that they had been notified before giving bail of the names under which they had been indicted, and had voluntarily given bail under those indictments, and that the witnesses were in court ready to identify them.

The reader will look in vain for an answer to the question, "Why were not these men required to plead, under the provisions of Section 277 of the Code, above cited?"

FARCE NO. III.

July 9, 1884, the Sheriff of Kings County visited the office of the New York Society for the Suppression of Vice, and with a great show of zeal was very anxious to be informed where the men could be found for whom he held bench warrants, he having fourteen warrants with him for these men. He was referred to the bail-bonds and told that the men he wanted had appeared, and were then under bail, with the exception of two, who had availed themselves of the information that they had been indicted and had failed to appear. These two have not been arrested down to the present time, although one of them was and is within the reach of the District Attorney, if he had chosen to call or chooses now to call him into court. One of them, Michael J. Kelly, was indicted and arrested September, 1883, for offences committed at Brighton Beach race track, and is under bonds to appear under that indictment. He could any day have been called, if the District Attorney had chosen, and made to appear in court, or his former bond have been forfeited.

July 1, 1884, Mr. Ridgway was informed by the writer that the party indicted as Michael J. Kelly, June 30, 1884, was the same man who had been indicted in September, 1883, and was then under bonds as Michael J. Tully.

A request was then made of Mr. Ridgway to have the old indictment called for trial, in order to bring the defendant into court, where he could be easily identified by the witnesses and apprehended by the Sheriff on the bench warrant. This has not been done.

LATER.—November 20, 1884, the following letter was written to Mr. Ridgway, and at 3:45 P. M. on that date was delivered at his office by Mr. George E. Oram :

Hon. JAMES W. RIDGWAY,
         District Attorney, County of Kings,
              Brooklyn, N. Y.

     *   *   *   *   *   *   *   *   *   *   *   *

There is another bench warrant (or should be one) which I explained to you July 1, 1884, for the arrest of Michael J. Kelly, indicted June last for violating Section 351 of Chapter IX. of the Penal Code, which ought to have been executed a long time ago, but which has not been thus far. July 1 I informed you that this man Kelly had been indicted in Kings County, for a similar offence, in September, 1883; that he was then arrested and under bonds in your court for trial ; and that if you would call that case up for trial, the said Kelly could then be arrested on said bench warrant. For reasons best known to yourself, this old case has not been called once for trial since you have been in office, and the bench warrant has not been executed. He was indicted for selling French pools. Will you please have the old case called for trial, the present bench warrant executed and the said Kelly held for trial on the indictment found in June last ?

This man Kelly, I am informed, has continued in the business since June at Coney Island, violating the same law. I remain,
                         Respectfully yours,
                    (Signed) ANTHONY COMSTOCK,
                         Secretary and Chief Special Agent.

Nothing has been done to date.

This letter was called forth by Mr. Ridgway's conduct in court a day or two previous thereto.

A bench warrant had previously been placed in our hands for execution against a notorious gambler who had formerly been engaged plying his traffic at Coney Island. We found that this party had gone to his home in Chicago, Ill., and we held the warrant, pending his return.

Mr. Ridgway called Mr. Britton, one of our witnesses, before the bar of the court and in a loud and insulting tone of voice demanded the return of the warrant.   Mr. Britton, taken by surprise, as no intimation had ever been given that the warrant was wanted, stood confused, not knowing at first what to say.   Mr. Ridgway then, in an excited manner, ap- pealed to the Court for an order to oblige Mr. Britton to turn over the warrant.   The Court refused to so order, and for once Mr. Ridgway was left unsupported.   This letter returned the warrant called for by him, and then called attention to a certain other bench warrant issued by Ridgway to the Sheriff which had not been served upon Michael J. Kelly, one of the two indicted gamblers who had not responded to the polite attention shown the fraternity by the District At- torney June 30, 1884.

This circumstance simply shows the difference between the treatment which honest men and gamblers received at Mr Ridgway's hands.   Our crime was that we demanded the proper enforcement of the law against gamblers.

CHAPTER VI.

FARCE NO. IV.

An Innocent Man Arrested and Held to Bail.

JULY 11, 1884, or three days after John T. McDougall had demurred * as aforesaid, a most remarkable transaction

---

* Just here a word of explanation is necessary. The writer, July 8, 1884, sat in court with pencil and paper, and, as each one of the defendants was called, recorded the action taken in each case, then afterwards went to the Clerk of the Court and, in order to be correct, received from the Clerk a memorandum of the action taken in each case, showing that the demurrer was entered by counsel to this indictment, July 8, 1884.

As confirmatory of what I state I quote from the Brooklyn *Eagle* of July 8, 1884, as follows :—

"Mr. Wernberg then demurred to the following names : John Kelly, Thomas Murray, David Johnson, James Dunn, *Dougal McDougall*, Alfred Cridge, Michael Murray, John Stow, and James E. Kelly."

The Brooklyn *Union* of the same date says on this point :

"The names were called and demurrers entered in the case of Alfred Cridge, James E. Kelly, Thomas Murray, John S. Stow, David Johnson, *Dougal McDougall*, John Kelly, James Dunn, and Michael Murray,"

and then presents a list of names against whom bench warrants were issued.

These names were the names given in the indictments, and were the titles of the cases.

A few days ago (Feb., 1887), on receiving a certified copy of the record of the Court, we found that that shows that McDougall's demur was entered as having been made July 15, 1884. July 15, 1884, these cases were to have come up, on argument on the demurrers. We were in court when court opened, and were informed that all the cases had occurred in Judge Moore's chambers, in the rear of the Sessions Court Clerk's office.

The sheriff arraigned two men before Judge Moore whom he had arrested upon two of the fourteen bench warrants. One of these gave the name of Martin Jordan. He had previously, June 30, 1884, voluntarily appeared in Mr. Ridgway's office and given bail. He had been indicted as Mark Jordan, and gave bail accordingly on said indictment, both names being set out in the bail-bond. They were about to require another bond, when their attention was called to the fact that Jordan had already given bail, as aforesaid, and he was allowed to go.

Not so the other man. Dougal McDougall was innocent. And yet, notwithstanding that he was innocent, and that John T. McDougall, the real culprit, had voluntarily appeared and given bail June 30, 1884, and that the bail-bond had been sent for and then and there examined by Judge Moore and Mr. Jenks (said bail-bond reading as follows, to wit :—" An indictment having been found on the 30th day of June, in the Court of Sessions of Kings County, charging Dougal McDougall, whose true name is John McDougall, with the crime of recording bets and wagers," and signed " John T. McDougall " [John T. gave his residence in this bond as Hoboken, N. J.]) ; notwithstanding that the writer, who was present, with Mr. George E. Oram, one of the principal witnesses, publicly informed Judge Moore and Mr. Jenks that the man who had given bail June 30 was the *right man ;* that the one then and there present calling himself Dougal

---

been adjourned. The writer waited awhile, then returned to New York leaving two witnesses to watch if any of our cases came up. They reported that none were called.

Query: Why was not the demur entered on the minutes of the court on the 8th of July, 1884? How did it come to be entered July 15? Was it an oversight?

McDougall, whose residence was given as 275 Hudson Ave.,
New York, was *not* the man ; that he was innocent, and
"not the one the witnesses had testified against before the
Grand Jury, not the man indicted, and that one of the witnesses, Mr. George E. Oram, then present, would so swear";
notwithstanding the further fact that but three days before
the said John T. McDougall had before Judge Moore, by
counsel, demurred to the indictment, thus in law admitting
all of the facts to be true—yet, despite all, Dougal McDougall, of New York, the innocent man, was held in bail upon
this indictment against John T. McDougall of Hoboken,
N. J., the guilty party.

After John T. McDougall had given bail June 30 (we
met him coming out of Mr. Ridgway's office), he returned to
his gambling business. He was found there the same day,
again violating the law, when the officer sent by Mr. Ridgway arrived (with Mr. Britton and the *Union* reporter) to
notify his associates,—two gamblers who had been jointly
indicted with him,—that they had been indicted, and requested them to appear and give bail the next morning.

The next morning he (John T.) appeared with his associates, and was with them when they gave bail. The witnesses saw them together at the race course the day they
secured the evidence upon which they had been indicted,
and we all saw them again July 1, when John T. brought his
associates to give bail for them.

Every effort was made upon our part to prevent such an
outrage upon law and justice. We received for our pains a
severe rebuke from the judge and slurring attacks from the
press.

The same afternoon the Brooklyn *Union* came out with an
article headed : " Pool Humbug—The Wrong Men Indicted
and the Wrong Men Arrested—Two Pool-sellers Arrested
in New York on Bench Warrants—Anthony Comstock's Futile Attempt to Convince Judge Moore that He was Proceed-

ing Wrongly in the Matter, but the Judge Sits Down on Comstock and Peremptorily Closes the Discussion. "

We must now record a fact which we sincerely regret to be obliged to present ; but we record facts, and if we would be faithful, we must present them as they exist.

WAS JUDGE MOORE ADVISED OF THE FACTS ?

A few moments before eight o'clock on that morning, July 11, 1884, the following letter was left for him at his residence, Washington Avenue, Brooklyn, by Mr. G. E. Oram. Mr. Oram reported in writing to delivering this letter at 20 minutes before 8 o'clock July 11, 1884. Read this carefully.

LETTER, JULY 10, 1884, TO JUDGE HENRY A. MOORE.

July 10, 1884.

Hon. HENRY A. MOORE,
      County Judge,
          Washington Avenue,
             Brooklyn, N. Y.

Dear Sir :—As a friend of the court, I am advised to present the following facts for your information :

Statements have been made in open court before your Honor, and, so far as I have heard, not contradicted, that men have been arrested and required to give bail in certain indictments found by the last Grand Jury for violation of Section 351 of the Penal Code other than the ones indicted by the Grand Jury.

The facts are as follows, and are susceptible of proof by three witnesses at least :

On the 30th of June the Grand Jury filed indictments against twenty-two different persons.

The same day, immediately upon the filing of said indictments, certain persons came forward and at once gave bail without being arrested upon any warrant, as I am informed, to wit : Albert H. Cridge, David J. Johnson, Dougal McDougall, Mark Jordan, James E. Kelly, John S. Stow, Thomas Murray, James Dunn, and Michael Murray. Also, one John Kelly.

The afternoon of the same day, by direction of the District Attorney, persons were sent to the race track at Sheepshead Bay, where these men who had been indicted by the Grand Jury were actually engaged in violating the law, with a list containing the names of persons indicted, these names having been furnished the Grand Jury by the witnesses as the names by which these men were known to the witnesses.

One of the assistants in the District Attorney's office had this list of names.

Mr. Britton, one of the witnesses before the Grand Jury, upon whose testimony these indictments were found, went with the officers of the District Attorney s office and personally pointed out the men whom he had testified against before the Grand Jury, and against whom these indictments had been found, and they were then and there notified that they had been indicted under certain names then given them.

The men thus identified were in the very booths and committing the very crimes for which they had been indicted, occupying the very places and conducting the very same kind of business which they had been indicted for committing on the dates set out.in the several indictments. The parties so notified appeared the next morning voluntarily and gave bail to the indictments, before giving bail, however, being informed that they had been indicted as follows, to wit:

A person giving the name of William Warring was the person identified, known, and indicted as Peter Cridge, and gave bail under that indictment.   .

The man giving the name of William McNamara was the man indicted and known to the witnesses as Frederick Dutch, and the person against whom the witnesses gave their testimony before the Grand Jury. He gave bail also.

The same is true of the following parties, the first name being the name set out in the indictment and the last name the names which they claim as their correct names, but which was not known to the witnesses until after they had been notified that they had been indicted under the name set out in the indictments, to wit:

Aaron Platt, alias John White.

Herman Schneider, alias Frank Snyder,

George Rose,	"	James Fry,
John Kelly,	"	F. Rodman,
John Smith,	"	F. T. Bradley,
Richard Baker,	"	T. J. Meehan,
Charles Kimball,	"	Daniel Wartzfelder,
George Hall,	"	James Varley,
Andrew Fuller,	"	Daniel Gleason.

These men, except Wartzfelder, Rodman, and Fry, were all before your Honor on Tuesday last. The witnesses were also present who could have identified them to the court as the men actually indicted by the Grand Jury, and as being known to the witnesses as the persons under the names set out in the indictments. These were the only names by which these men were known to the witnesses until after they had been indicted, and notified that they had been indicted under the names set out in the several indictments.

A man was indicted with Dougal M°cDougall known to the witnesses as John Kelly. Some man claiming to be named John Kelly, but employed by some other person, and in no way connected with Dougal McDougall, was allowed to give bail upon this indictment in the District Attorney's office as soon as the indictments were filed, without being identified, or an opportunity given the witnesses to identify him, as the proper man. But the witness in the presence of the officers from the District Attorney's office, who went down to where these men were violating the laws on the first day of July, identified a man who gave the name of F. Rodman as the man that was known to the witnesses, and the man against whom they testified before the Grand Jury as John Kelly. And F. Rodman, as I am informed, has since appeared and given bail upon this indictment in the sum of $1000.

Yesterday the Sheriff came with fourteen bench warrants to my office in New York to know the whereabouts of these men. I was obliged to say to the Sheriff that the men that were sitting in court on the 8th inst., after having given bail under each of these indictments, were the only ones known to us as the persons wanted upon those bench warrants. As the *People* took no cognizance of the fact that these men were in court, and as the bail was not forfeited, I could only send him to the men actually under bail, and the only ones wanted under these indictments, as they are the only men indicted by the Grand Jury.

I can only add that the object of this letter is simply to advise the Court of the facts in the premises.

To show the Court that there can be no mistake in this matter (if the men identified by the witness as the persons wanted are the same who gave bail), I have simply to present the simple fact that the persons who were actually engaged in violating the law upon the dates the three witnesses were present at Sheepshead Bay and obtained the evidence against them upon which the Grand Jury indicted them, that on the thirtieth day of June these same men were in the same sheds or stalls engaged in the same unlawful business, when the witness identified them to the officers of the District Attorney's office, and these officers notified each of them that they had been indicted under the names set opposite their names in this letter, and the names which they appeared of their own free will and gave bail to on the indictments the next morning.

The men who gave bail on the various indictments now before the court are, so far as the witnesses have been permitted to see them, the identical men indicted and called for in the indictments.

I have the honor to be,

Very respectfully, sir,

Your obedient servant,

(Signed) ANTHONY COMSTOCK,

Sec'y.

In this letter, there having been but one McDougall (John T.) under bail, we used the names set out in the title of the case, as is customary in referring to a defendant under indictment.

It will be seen by the foregoing letter that Judge Moore was informed of the irregular conduct of the District Attorney in protecting these gamblers by sending men to the race track, and instead of arresting, notifying them of the action of the Grand Jury before they were arrested, in violation of the Code. He was informed of the fact that the law was being openly violated in the presence of the officers of his court or District Attorney's office. He was clearly informed of the specific crimes that were then being committed, of the particular manner in which these men had been indicted, as well as the farce that had been enacted before him July 8, when the District Attorney's assistant, Mr. Jenks, remained mute and allowed these men to sit there in contempt of the proceedings of the court, without obliging them to come forward and plead to the indictments to which they had voluntarily given bail as the right parties when they were called. These facts were faithfully presented to Judge Moore, and if no action was taken upon them, certainly the one who communicated those facts to the learned judge cannot be blamed by him.

And to further show the good faith of the agents of the Society for the Suppression of Vice, and the faithful manner in which they have followed up these cases, read the following letter addressed to Judge Moore the same day, after he "sits down on Comstock and peremptorily closes the discussion."

This letter is worthy of more than passing notice. A careful reading will throw a strong light upon the history of these gambling cases, particularly the McDougall case. The effort to inform Judge Moore was falsely characterized as an attempt to dictate to the judge.

July 11, 1884.

Hon. HENRY A. MOORE,
    County Judge,
        451 Washington Ave.,
            Brooklyn, N. Y.

Sir :—

I most respectfully present to you that you do me a great injustice by charging me with attempting to dictate to you or any one else in the cases brought before you this morning. I, on the contrary, had no such thought or intention. I thought you were not acquainted with the facts in these cases. *In the case of Mark Jordan and the case of Dougal McDougall the men actually indicted appeared voluntarily, and gave bail a very few moments after the indictments were filed.* They knew that they were engaged committing the very offences for which they were charged in the indictment, and to prevent any interference with their unlawful business, the principal men engaged openly in violating the laws at Sheepshead Bay race course stood, as it were, waiting with their bondsmen ready to give bail upon these indictments as soon as the indictments were filed. They virtually admitted that they were the men wanted, and were on hand before bench warrants could have been issued (unless they were drawn before the indictments were filed), ready to admit themselves as the men called for in the indictments, and gave bail accordingly.

Again, the same afternoon, Mr. Britton went down with officers to the pool-stands, where the laws were openly violated, and these persons' unlawful business was interrupted long enough to enable the officers to notify those who had not given bail that they had been indicted, and they were then and there told what names they had been indicted under, and the next morning these men *voluntarily* appeared and *voluntarily* gave bail.

After all this, they come into court and try to befog and deceive the Court and make it appear they have been arrested wrongfully.

Your manner would indicate that I was doing some great wrong in thus addressing you. With great respect to the Court, permit me to say that any citizen has a right to see that the laws are properly enforced, and if one sees a court or judge being imposed upon, as I felt you were being, it seemed to me not wrong or improper for such a one to respectfully call attention to the facts.

Again, I have always understood that any person, however high in authority, could be approached by a citizen, however lowly, especially where it is a matter involving the integrity and good name of an entire State, and upon this theory I thought I had the right to address you in this particular. Laws are openly and flagrantly violated in Kings County by gamblers and pool-sellers, and have been for more than three years. Scores of indictments have been ordered by the Grand Jury and never tried, notwithstanding in the majority of cases the evidence is positive of the defendants' guilt. Gamblers from New York City, New Jersey, Pennsylvania, men in some instances who have been convicted and sentenced for similar offences in other parts of the State, are permitted to come to Brooklyn and Kings County and openly set at defiance the laws of the State. Out of over fifty indictments in your court, all but two or three have been dismissed without a trial, when there has been positive evidence of guilt.

For instance, David Philipps was arrested June 22, 1883, charged with selling lottery policies; was indicted Sept., 1883, and the indictment dismissed without trial Dec., 1883, notwithstanding there were two witnesses to prove tha the sold the slip, backed by the manifold-book upon which the policy was recorded, which was seized on him at the time of arrest, and upon which he was entering lottery policies when arrested. This man, when arrested, was a special policeman, and we found his badge upon him.

The same day Maurice Foster was also arrested, and the facts are precisely the same, except that he was not a policeman. His case was never tried, but summarily dismissed after indictment.

Indictments against a number of men who, after being arrested and indicted once, continued on in the policy business, again arrested and indicted, were also summarily dismissed last December. I repeat, over fifty such indictments were never brought to trial, but, supported by absolute and positive evidence of guilt, were dismissed.

Last year scores of gamblers, throughout the season, openly defied the laws of this State in Kings County, and after much opposition in the District Attorney's office I at last secured the indictment and arrest of a large number; yet not one of those cases has ever been tried. I am quite aware that a court cannot try criminals without the cases are brought before it for trial, and that ordinarily the District Attorney is the one to present these matters to the Court, but there are times when a citizen may speak to the Court and appeal to the Court.

I have repeatedly defended your Honor's name from reproach, and defended you when I have heard you censured because the laws against these gambling schemes had not been enforced, by saying that " the trouble has been that they take good care not to allow their cases to come before the Court."

I do not believe, and never have believed, that your Honor would permit your court to be used as a protection or cover for criminals, nor that you would allow the laws to be enforced in the interest of crime or so as to encourage those who make a business of violating the law, and because of my confidence, notwithstanding the rebuffs you have recently seen fit to give me, is the reason why I presented simply facts to your Honor.

I have earnestly and faithfully sought to enforce the law in a legal manner. I have found tremendous opposition. I am neither dismayed nor do I despair. I expect to live to see the laws enforced in Kings County against gamblers, and I believe they would be if the cases could but be properly placed before the court and jury.

It is claimed outside that nothing can or will be done ; that no matter what the evidence is, these cases will be tried the same as the others have been.

Now, Judge Moore, do you wonder I earnestly sought to reach you, in view of all that has taken place in the past? With the claims of the gamblers and their friends of the present, do I err in coming to a magistrate in whom I had confidence and pleading for an opportunity to present the facts?

I am frank to say the trouble in the past in bringing these criminals to justice, in securing the enforcement of the laws against gambling, and in checking the open, bold, and defiant violation of these laws, has not been from the fraternity of gamblers, but in the District Attorney's office. In these very cases it was charged by rumor that there had been a contract made that no person should be arrested nor any of their unlawful paraphernalia seized. This rumor I personally informed Mr. Ridgway of, and, notwithstanding it, his officer who had the bench warrant (as he informed me) visited the men indicted while they were actually engaged violating the very law under which they had severally been indicted. Yet none were arrested; the unlawful business was not interfered with, except interrupted long enough to notify them that they had been indicted,

6

and inform them of the name under which they had been indicted, and that they could come and give bail the next day in the forenoon (at an hour when there was no pool-selling, so that their unlawful traffic should not in any way be inconvenienced or interrupted by the enforcement of the law). All but one of these men voluntarily came to the District Attorney's office, as I am informed, the next day, and in presence of their counsel voluntarily gave bail, none of them raising a single objection, that I heard, that they were not the persons indicted, and I was present when they signed their bonds. These men sat in your presence when their cases were called, and witnesses were there to identify them. Yet none of these facts are laid before the Court—not a word of remonstrance said on behalf of the people—while the claim is falsely made that none of these men are the parties indicted. I, knowing to the contrary, felt it my duty to bring the matter to your attention, and requested Mr. Jenks so to do, informing him of the presence of these men and the witnesses to identify them. The man McDougall, who was waiting to give bail when the indictment was filed, virtually admitted himself the guilty party. Again, Mr. Ridgway informed me that he had been advised that Mr. Kelly (the boss gambler) would produce every man indicted if we would identify them. Accordingly Mr. Britton, an eyewitness to the offences for which they had been indicted, went down to the gamblers' stands, and Mr. Kelly aforesaid very kindly went about with him and the District Attorney's officer, and these men were notified as aforesaid. Not one of these facts was presented to the Court. Is there any law to shut the mouth of a citizen intent upon the honest enforcement of these laws? I wot not.

During more than eleven years of experience in the courts I have frequently appeared before Judges of the Supreme Court of the United States sitting as U. S. Circuit Judges, and before Supreme Court Judges in various locations, and I have never been denied the right to present in a respectful manner whatever facts that pertained to the proper enforcement of the law. These high judges deemed it not improper to allow any citizen, however humble, to befriend the Court, and because of the uniform courtesy thus extended me in the honest efforts to secure justice and the proper enforcement of the laws, I thought I was not erring when, as a friend of the Court and back of a movement to enforce the laws, I brought to your Honor's mind the true facts in these cases.

I am not so weak minded as to presume to dictate to any Court, neither am I so cowardly as to shrink from any duty, unpleasant though it be, when duty calls. When I see the representatives of the people standing mute, and allowing gross misstatements to be made in the court, in cases where I am interested and in which my duty is involved,

I certainly shall endeavor in a proper manner to overcome the evil and make the facts known.

If you knew the wild excitement of these gambling games, the long list of complaints coming of youth ruined by these gambling schemes, of women and children robbed by these merciless devices to rob the poor and credulous to enrich a few bosses, the increasing demoralization from the non-enforcement of these and kindred laws, you would not be surprised or vexed that I stood on the alert and firm not to allow a single advantage to these criminals.

The importance of the subject, the record of past cases, and the injustice done me by misconception of facts, is my apology for thus trespassing upon your time at such length.

Knowing and believing that I am right in these matters, I desire to be fully understood, being assured that no honest man will find fault with a sincere and determined effort to secure the proper enforcement of law against a body of criminals banded together in Kings County to defy and transgress the law.

I certainly shall endeavor to conform to every rule laid down in your Honor's court, and if I should transgress, it will be from ignorance, and not from premeditation or with wilful intent.

I have the honor to be,
Very respectfully, sir,
Your obedient servant,
(Signed) ANTHONY COMSTOCK,
Secretary.

Nothing was done, so far as we can ascertain.

Having performed our duty faithfully, we felt that we had, at least, the right of self-defence, and also the right to present the facts so as to expose the unfaithfulness of those who evidently were deceiving the Court. Note the very full and earnest manner in which these facts were presented to this Court. It will be interesting, in following out the history of these cases, to bear in mind that an earnest protest had been made to the Court itself. The Court had been informed, whether he regarded the *facts* or not.

In presenting this correspondence it is done with feelings of sincere regret. The writer regretted the necessity of writing such a letter. He also regrets the necessity of now putting it in its place in the history of these gambling cases. If the facts had not been laid before the Court, then the blame might be attached to this organization ; but we submit that the candid reader must acknowledge that an honest and earnest effort was made on our part to secure the proper administration of justice in these cases. We did what we could to secure the prosecution of these much-protected gamblers.

This illustrates how easy it is for a prosecuting attorney to deceive and humbug a Court, make a defence for himself, and attempt to belittle those who dare to stand for truth and justice.

Doubtless Judge Moore had some reason why he did not investigate these matters and put the seal of condemnation of his Court upon them. It is possible that he, being the judge, with many other things upon his mind, may have forgotten them in the after history of the McDougall farce.

NOT SO MR. RIDGWAY.

After writing Judge Moore, the matter was again brought to the attention of Mr. Ridgway, both by letter and affidavit, which were delivered to him personally.

IS THERE ANY EXCUSE FOR MR. RIDGWAY?

To demonstrate Mr. Ridgway's knowledge, and show the public that he is without excuse, we present the following letter, sent to Mr. Ridgway July 16, 1884, to wit :—

NEW YORK, *July* 16, 1884.

Hon. JAMES A. RIDGWAY,
          District Attorney Kings Co.,
                    Brooklyn, N. Y.
Dear Sir :

Enclosed herewith please find affidavits identifying parties in the following cases, to wit :

The People,
     vs.
Dougal McDougall, who says his right name is John T. McDougall,

George Rose, who says his right name is James Fry,
John Kelly, " " " " " " Frank Rodman.
    The People,
    vs.
David J. Johnson,
John Smith, who says his right name is F. K. Bradley,
Richard Baker, " " " " " T. J. Meehan.
    The People,
    vs.
Albert H. Cridge,
Peter Cridge, who says his right name is Wm. Warring,
Frederick Dutch, " " " " Wm. McNamara.
    The People,
    vs.
Mark Jordan, who says his right name is Martin Jordan,
Aaron Platt, " " " " " John White,
Herman Schneider, " " " " Frank Snyder.
    The People,
    vs.
James E. Kelly,
John S. Stow,
Thomas Murray,
Andrew Fuller, who says his right name is Daniel Gleason
    The People,
    vs.
Michael Murray,
Charles Kimball, who says his right name is Daniel Wartzfelder,
George Hall, " " " " " James Varley.

Very truly yours,

(Signed) ANTHONY COMSTOCK,

Secretary,

Per D.

Let it be observed that the names first used are the only names in the indictments of June 30, and as there were no other indictments against these parties when this letter and affidavit were written, we used the title of the case as set out in the indictment. So in speaking of Dougal McDougall, who says his right name is John T. McDougall, reference is had to the person who gave bail June 30, and the quotation is taken from his bond. It is more clearly stated in the following affidavit, which was one of several enclosed in this letter.

The affidavit read as follows, setting out the title of the case as per the indictment of June 30, 1884, to wit :—

COURT OF SESSIONS, COUNTY OF KINGS.

THE PEOPLE
vs.
DOUGAL McDOUGALL,
GEORGE ROSE, AND
JOHN KELLY.
City of Brooklyn, County of Kings,   ss.
and State of New York.

Joseph A. Britton, being of full age, of 150 Nassau Street, New York City, being duly sworn, deposes and says, that he was a witness before the Grand Jury in the above entitled case, and gave testimony against a person then known to him as Dougal McDougall aforesaid, whom deponent had personally seen at Sheepshead Bay violating Chapter (9) Nine of the Penal Code of the State of New York, as is more particularly described in the indictment filed June 30, 1884, in the above entitled case.

Deponent is informed that the person known to deponent as Dougal McDougall appeared at the District Attorney's office, of his own volition, on the 30th day of June, 1884, and gave bail for his appearance upon said indictment upon the morning of the 30th day of June, immediately upon the filing of the indictment, and *then claimed his right name was John T. McDougall.*

Deponent further says, on the afternoon of the same day he personally visited the place where the said McDougall had previously been seen by deponent violating the law upon the date complained of, and after the said McDougall had given bail as aforesaid, saw him engaging in the same business, and with him the said George Rose, who then gave his right name as James Fry, and the said John Kelly, who also gave his name as Frank Rodman, and the last two were then and there acting with the said McDougall as upon previous occasions as specified in said indictment.

Deponent further says, that afterwards, on the first day of July, 1884, the said Dougal McDougall, alias John T. McDougall, appeared again, accompanied by the said George Rose, alias James Fry, and John Kelly, alias Frank Rodman, when they appeared voluntarily, and gave bail upon said indictment; and the said Dougal McDougall, now known as John T. McDougall, and George Rose, now known as James Fry, and John Kelly, now known as Frank Rodman, are the true and only individuals referred to in said indictments and against whom deponent and the other witness gave testimony before the Grand Jury on said complaint, as more particularly set forth in affidavit form as now filed with the District Attorney or under his control, upon which said indictment is found. Deponent had conversation with the said McDougall on the 1st day of July, as well as upon the former dates set out in this affidavit, and knows him by sight well, and knows that he is the man indicted and the man who committed the offence.

Subscribed and sworn to before me
this 16th day of July, 1884.

JOSEPH A. BRITTON.

W. C. BEECHER,
Notary Public.

Another affidavit filed in the same case, the same day, particularly referred to James Fry and Frank Rodman in connection with John T. McDougall.

Mr. Jere Wernberg, counsel, was a constant attendant upon these men as his clients, and was present when Mr. Britton identified them, June 30, to Mr. Ridgway's peace officer, and also when they gave bail. If these parties were not the right ones, why did he allow them to give bail? They were not under arrest or obliged to give bail unless they desired to do so.

July 18, 1884, to cure the defect in names, as it was claimed that some had been indicted under erroneous names, the witnesses were called before the Grand Jury, and those who sat mute July 8, by consent of Mr. Jenks, were re-indicted under the names which they had given when notified by Mr. Ridgway's peace officer, and under which they had given bail on the former indictment.

These bills were filed July 23, 1884.

John T. McDougall, James Fry, and Frank Rodman were
indicted in the new indictment as follows:—
    Title :—   "The People,
                        against
    " James Fry, alias George Rose.
    " Frank Rodman, alias John Kelly.
    " John T. McDougall, alias Dougal McDougall."
*Except the names, this indictment is word for word the same
as the indictment of June 30, 1880.*

The last names are the ones they were known by to the
witnesses previously to their indictment, June 30 ; the first
are, as they claimed, their right names.

None of those indicted July 23, 1884, were called upon to
plead until Dec. 1, 1884.

At that time Judge Moore overruled the demurs of July,
1884, and judgment of conviction was entered upon eleven
indictments, *one of the eleven being the McDougall* indictment
of June 30, 1884.

The writer and witnesses were all in court on this date,
December 1, 1884. After the demurrer had been entered the
Clerk of the Court called "John T. McDougall" to come
and plead to this second indictment of July 23, 1884. This
indictment, let it be remembered, was for the precise offence
that a judgment of conviction had just been entered against
John T. McDougall only a few moments before, under
the June 30 indictment. John T. did not respond. Again
the Clerk called, "John T. McDougall to the bar." Again
there was no response. Whereupon Mr. Ridgway took the
indictment and called "Dougal McDougall." To this
Dougal, the innocent, responded with alacrity. As he approached the bar the writer informed Mr. Ridgway that he
(Ridgway) was mistaken ; that this man Dougal was not the
party indicted, and that witnesses were then and there present to so swear, if he would call them.

Notwithstanding the statement made to Judge Moore

July 11, and letter of same date; the letter to Mr. Ridgway of July 16, with accompanying affiadvits; the demur of July 8; the judgment of conviction of even date (Dec. 1) against the right man, John T. McDougall—notwithstanding all these, James W. Ridgway insultingly replied to the offer to properly identify his man, arraigned Dougal McDougall, of New York, an innocent man, before Judge Moore in the Sessions Court, and obliged him to plead to an indictment found against John T. McDougall, of Hoboken, N. J., the real culprit, and then afterwards, to wit, Dec. 15, 1884, tried this same innocent man, upon this indictment, before Judge Moore and a jury, and the jury are reported as "rendering their verdict of not guilty without leaving their seats."

DID JUDGE MOORE KNOW?

Suppose he ignored our protest in his Chambers of July 11, 1884, and our letter of same date.

Dec. 1 John T. McDougall had had judgment of conviction entered against him on his demurrer. Within half an hour afterwards the Clerk of the Court called twice for "John T. McDougall" to come forward to plead to the second indictment, found against him under his right name, dated July 23, 1884. He does not respond. Mr. Ridgway in loud tones calls "Dougal McDougall" (the innocent), and arraigns him before Judge Moore to plead to an indictment against John T. McDougall, the man just convicted for the very same offence. No objection is made by the Court, although the man who had been held to bail against our protest July 11, 1884, was then and there substituted in open court. Dougal pleaded "not guilty," and Dec. 15 was named as a day for his trial.

ANOTHER FARCE.

Afterwards another funny thing was enacted. Dec. 3, 1884, John T. McDougall, of Hoboken, N. J., was obliged to

give bail upon this second indictment for the precise offence
for which he was then under judgment of conviction. Yet
he has not yet pleaded to this indictment. So much for
matters of record.

ANOTHER LETTER TO JUDGE MOORE.

Determined that Judge Moore should not be deceived,
Dec. 10, 1884, the following letter was left at his residence,
by Mr. George E. Oram, to wit:—

LETTER TO HENRY A. MOORE, DEC. 10, 1884.

December 10, 1884.
Hon. HENRY A. MOORE,
    Judge Kings County Court of Sessions,
        Brooklyn, N. Y.
Sir:

I deem it my duty as a friend of the Court to present the following
facts for your consideration and to further the ends of justice in Kings
County.

First. I enclose herewith the certified copy of sentences imposed upon the following named persons, whose cases are now before you upon
the indictments upon which judgment of conviction has been entered.
In each of these cases I was personally in court at time of sentence in
New York Court of Special Sessions, and know of my own knowledge
that the parties named in the indictments before your honorable Court
as James E. Kelly, John S. Stow, Thomas Murray, Michael Murray,
James Varley, and Daniel Wartzfelder are the same as were sentenced in
Special Sessions upon the dates set forth in the enclosed paper.

Second. On the very day on which James E. Kelly, John S. Stow, and
Thomas Murray were sentenced, upon their plea of guilty (June 16, 1884),
each of these men was found in the afternoon of the same day committing the same crimes at the town of Gravesend. Michael Murray and
the other two men had been arrested and held for trial, and their cases
had been before the court the same morning, and adjourned, and they
too were engaged in the same unlawful business as Kelly and Stow and
Murray, also at Gravesend, and Mr. Britton and two associates secured
the evidence of their guilt on the same afternoon.

Third. These men continued in the same unlawful business, and
openly defied the laws of the State, and James E. Kelly and Michael

Murray are each of them notorious offenders and are known as "boss gamblers." In September Messrs. J. A. Britton and George E. Oram, of this office, personally were present and saw these six men violating the law in the same manner and form as set out in the indictments now before your court.

Fourth. *The man whom Mr. Ridgway, District Attorney, called to plead upon the indictment found against John T. McDougall, alias Dougal McDougall, et al., is not the man indicted, nor the one against whom the witnesses gave testimony before either of the Grand Juries.*

June 30, the morning immediately following the filing of the indictments against pool gamblers at Gravesend, the "boss gamblers" voluntarily appeared and gave bail. This haste was presumably to prevent any arrest during pool-selling hours, as they went right from the court to their unlawful business. The man indicted as Dougal McDougall gave his right name as John T. McDougall, and this man is, as far as any of the witnesses know, the only man known in these indictments, or as doing business at Gravesend in June last, by the name of McDougall. He was the "boss" of his booth or place, and an affidavit was filed in Mr. Ridgway's office July last certifying to that fact. After filing the affidavit, the July Grand Jury called the witnesses before them, and John T. McDougall, the man who voluntarily gave bail June 30, 1884, was reindicted. This man, John T. McDougall, further appeared July 1, 1884, in the District Attorney's office, with his assistants, James Fry and Frank Rodman, when they gave bail under the names under which they were indicted. Frank Rodman was known to the witnesses first as John Kelly, and was so indicted, was notified by an officer while engaged carrying on pool-selling June 30, 1884, that he had been indicted as John Kelly, and voluntarily appeared the next morning, July 1, 1884, and gave bail as the one indicted as John Kelly; and since then, in July, 1884, the July Grand Jury have, as I understand, found new indictments against him in his own right name, or the name he says is his right name.

But please take notice that in the mean time the zeal to give bail on behalf of the gamblers was so great that some other person, known as John Kelly or calling himself as such, voluntarily went to the District Attorney's office and was there permitted to give bail on this same indictment. This man is unknown to the witnesses, and was not in any manner testified against before the Grand Jury by either of them, as you will find by examining them.

These facts have all been laid in writing before Mr. Ridgway, and yet for some reason he chooses to arraign Dougal McDougall, instead of John T. McDougall, upon an indictment found expressly against John

T. McDougall, and after he had given his right name, and after Mr. Ridgway knew the above facts.

Again, the man identified as Herman Schneider, afterwards indicted as Frank Snyder in July.   I am informed that a person other than the one pointed out and indicted as Snyder has been brought in by James E. Kelly and has entered bail upon said indictment.   The man which the witnesses knew and identified as Herman Schneider, and afterward knew as Frank Snyder, is described by each of them as a Jew, with black hair and mustache, and who wore a brown derby hat, drab lawn-tennis shirt, and is about twenty-eight years of age.

The man Snyder who appeared before your Honor Dec. 1, and pleaded "not guilty," is not the man.   He came afterwards to me and informed me that he came and gave bail because Kelly told him to; that he was not down to Gravesend and never saw Mr. Britton.   Mr. Britton went with the officers June 30 (whom Mr. Ridgway sent to notify the gamblers, while they were actually violating the laws, that they had been indicted), and says he identified the man above described.

I regret to add that the feeling in the District Attorney's office is such that I cannot hope to get these facts before your Honor; and yet believing your Honor desires all the light from any source you can get, to further the ends of justice and to properly enforce the laws, I deemed these facts of sufficient importance to warrant this intrusion upon your time and attention.   Please pardon my intrusion and believe me,

Very respectfully, sir,

Your obedient servant,

(Signed)   ANTHONY COMSTOCK,

Sec'y and Chief Special Agent.

Another letter was sent Mr. Ridgway in reference to Snyder, which we present.   Notwithstanding this letter and the one to Judge Moore, a man other than the one indicted and thus minutely described in each letter was tried in place of the guilty party.

LETTER TO MR. RIDGWAY, DECEMBER 12, 1884.

(Dictated.)

December 12, 1884.

Hon. JAMES W. RIDGWAY,

District Attorney,

Brooklyn, N. Y.

Sir:

My assistants having received subpœnas to appear in the trial of

Frank Snyder *et al.*, on Monday, I beg to state to you that the man indicted as Frank Snyder is a man of a Jewish cast, black or dark hair and mustache, about twenty-eight years of age; while the man Snyder, whom you arraigned to plead on the first of this month was not the man indicted, nor the man identified by Mr. Britton, as he has light hair and light mustache.

After the proceedings on the first day of December last, Mr. Snyder whom you arraigned to plead came outside of the court room and wanted to know what he had been indicted for, saying he had never been to the Sheepshead Bay race track, had never seen Mr. Britton, and that all he knew about it was that James E. Kelly (the boss gambler) told him to come up and give bail, and he came to the District Attorney's office and gave bail.

You will kindly observe that this could not have occurred if the bench warrants had been executed against the men whom Mr. Britton identified at the time they were violating the law at Sheepshead Bay on the thirtieth day of June, when he pointed them out to the officers whom you sent.

You will please take notice that J. G. K. Lawrence, secretary of the Coney Island Jockey Club, and Mr. Caldwell, the starter, whose initials I believe are J. F., are material witnesses to prove that the particular horses ran in the races in which the pools were sold, and I am informed that you cannot go safely to trial in the absence of these material witnesses.

Respectfully yours,

(Signed) ANTHONY COMSTOCK,

Secretary,

Per D.

Were they deceived, or could they not tell the difference between the men described in my letter? Did we perform our part faithfully or not?

Notwithstanding all, Dougal, the innocent, of New York, was tried in place of John T., the guilty, of Hoboken, N. J., before Judge Moore and a jury Dec. 15, 1884. So far as known, John T. has never yet been arraigned to plead to his last indictment. After Dougal pleaded, Dec 1., John T. appeared and gave bail on the same indictment Dec. 3, 1884; yet Dougal was tried in place of John, Dec 15.

" Barkis was willing." Why? Dougal was not friendly to our Society. He had been knocked out of a very profitable business in New York, been indicted, and pleaded "guilty " to two indictments in the General Sessions Court of New York City, been sentenced to pay a fine on one, and judgment, pending good behavior, had been suspended on the other. John T. was his brother, or so stated. It was natural for him to sympathize with his brother. The important thing, then, was to discredit the writer and turn the tables upon him. " Anything to beat the efforts of the Society for Suppression of Vice," seemed to be the cry.

Dougal knew, doubtless, that he was in good hands. He and his counsel cheerfully acquiesced in the plans of the prosecuting attorney, as neither of them made any protest or objection to Dougal's pleading to this indictment against John T., his brother. The Court turned a deaf ear to the facts in our letter of Dec. 10. The gamblers were jubilant. This was almost as good sport to them as "improving the breed of horses " by their favorite plan.

Was there an agreement to protect gamblers at Sheepshead Bay during 1884 ?

Was James E. Kelly, boss gambler, a false prophet when he said on June 30, " The Grand Jury will adjourn and these indictments will be pigeon-holed " ?

Lest the reader may be skeptical as to the possibility of such an outrage occurring in a Court of Justice in this country, I desire to emphasize the fact that the writer was present, saw and heard for himself, prepared the letters and affidavits, and now has beside him certified copies of the indictments, the John T. McDougall bail-bonds, and extracts from the minutes of the Court where Dougal, the innocent, was tried in the place of John T., the guilty.

STILL A GREATER SURPRISE.

The science of justice by the gambling method is almost on a par with the Kings County system of "improving the breed of horses."

The foregoing facts, I protest, are facts, and I hold myself ready to prove the same before Governor, Legislative Committee, or public.

While preparing this chapter there was served upon the writer, at 4.30 P. M., Jan. 28, 1887, a copy of Mr. Ridgway's answer to our charges against him before the Governor of the State, sworn to before his Chief Clerk, Mr. Walkley.

In his answer to Specification 1, Charge 4, which alleges the above facts, Mr. Ridgway presents the following as his sworn answer.

I present the affidavit first, as signed by him, which appears at the close of his remarkable document, so that the reader may see another one of his oaths, and give his answer the benefit of reading it through the sworn instrument which he has appended to give force and weight to what he says.

MR. RIDGWAY SWEARS.

The respondent, James W. Ridgway, above named, being duly sworn, deposes and says, that the foregoing answer is true of his own knowledge, except as to matters therein stated or alleged upon information and belief, and as to those matters he believes the same to be true.

JAMES W. RIDGWAY.

Sworn to before me this 24th
    day of January, 1887.

    A. H. WALKLEY,
      Notary Public,
        Kings County.

Read his version. He has my gratitude for his answer. Can anything be worse evidence against him than his own oath, in face of the facts?

He says :

CHARGE 4.

In answer to Specification 1 of Charge 4 : " Respondent avers that one John McDougall was indicted by the Grand Jury on the testimony of the officers acting with, and agents for, Anthony Comstock; that when said officers appeared before the Grand Jury they testified that they did not know whether said McDougall's name was John T. McDougall or Dugold McDougall; whereupon the Grand Jury found a bill against John T. McDougall, alias Dugold McDougall, and John T. McDougall appeared and gave bail on such indictment, and at the time he gave bail, the witness who testified against him in the Grand Jury room was present in the District Attorney's office and identified him as the person he had testified against; that thereafter John T. McDougall was taken before the Court of Sessions to plead to such indictment, and he then and there claimed to be innocent, and that said witness again identified him as the person against whom he had testified; that said McDougall insisted upon being tried before a jury, and was thereupon notified for trial ; that before the day of trial respondent was notified that the officers of said Society for the Suppression of Vice had been in consultation with said defendant since his arrest, and had agreed with said defendant that they would testify upon his trial that he was not the person that they had seen violate the law, that respondent, believing that said officers were acting corruptly, and intending to test the truth of such belief, insisted that said defendant should be tried in open court before a jury; that said officers, having a knowledge of that fact, wrote to respondent insisting that said McDougall was not the person; whereupon respondent placed said McDougall on trial, and called the witnesses who had testified against him before the Grand Jury, who were sworn, and under oath declared that they had never seen said McDougall on the race track ; whereupon said McDougall was acquitted; that thereafter the Grand Jury found an indictment against one Dugold McDougall, who was convicted under said indictment, in the Court of Sessions of the County of Kings."

The statements aforesaid are false. The witnesses identified these men, as already stated aforesaid by letters, affida-

vits, etc. Dougal was not "thereafter indicted and convicted." There were but two indictments : one of June 30, 1884,
and the other July 23, 1884, and both for the same offence
and against one and the same man. What reckless swearing
on Mr. Ridgway's part ! This is the man who asks the public to accept his word and oath as against that of the writer,
backed as the writer is by all the documentary evidence produced. Again he says, in answer to Specification 4 of
Charge 4 :—

"Respondent denies that he wilfully and deliberately substituted one
defendant for another, and avers that he was not acquainted either
with John T. McDougall or Dugold McDougall, and that he relied
for identification upon the officers of the Society for the Suppression
of Vice, and that the same man whom said officers identified, and who
appeared and gave bail, and who plead and was again identified in open
court, was the same man that respondent placed upon trial, and was
the same man who was acquitted, and whom it is alleged was an innocent man substituted for a guilty one."

Read the letters of July 16 ; the affidavits of same date ;
the demur of John T., July 8, 1884 ; the letters of July 10,
11, to Judge Henry A. Moore ; the protest before Judge
Moore of July 11 ; the attack of the public press upon
deponent: then consult the records of the Court, the bail-
bonds, the indictments, and see if there is a single word of
truth in the statements made by Mr. Ridgway under his
oath in the answer aforesaid.

Passing over much else in his answer that is false and mis-
leading, we quote concerning a subject of which the public
have at least some knowledge. He swears :

"When the public press was discussing the probabilities of respondent's renomination to the office of District Attorney, said Comstock
again preferred such charges, doubtless for the purpose of influencing
the public mind against respondent; that said Comstock has caused
to be published more than fifty times the matters embraced in these
specifications, and the matter has been thoroughly discussed from the
pulpit and public press and in public halls in the County of Kings, and

7

the charges so preferred were made the sole and only planks in the platform upon which the gentleman who was nominated against respondent appealed to the suffrages of the people of the County of Kings; and it was then asserted by an opposing press, and re-echoed by the orators on the stump, that THIS WAS THE SOLE AND ONLY ISSUE BEFORE THE PEOPLE."

HAS MR. RIDGWAY FORGOTTEN

that at a meeting held November 4, 1886, of twenty-third warders, in Liberty Hall, Nostrand and Gates Avenues, he (Ridgway) delivered an address? In this address he is reported in various papers as saying, concerning Rev. Theo. L. Cuyler, D.D., who preached a sermon on temperance, as follows:

" Under the leadership of his little friend, Billy Goodrich, he opened his church last Sunday and preached that I was the friend of the wine-bibber, and in favor of opening the German gardens on Sunday and having a good time. That probably prejudiced me in the minds of some of those who listened. He was under the impression that his church contained all the voters of the city. Next morning I cut out that portion of his speech, had it printed, and had 50,000 copies of it distributed around the Eastern District, where all good German fellow-citizens live, and I carried the Sixth Ward by more than 600 majority. So the old gentleman, who thought he was doing me an injury, did me so much good. I take this opportunity of returning my sincere and heartfelt thanks."

Was gambling the only issue?
Again he swears:

" These charges were preferred before a committee of Christian ministers of the City of Brooklyn, and respondent appeared before that body and made answer to such charges: *that the charges are false and untrue, made without any hope or belief that they will be sustained or that judgment will be rendered against respondent,* but are made clearly for the purpose of influencing a certain class of people upon whom complainant depends for his livelihood."

Read what the Christian ministers above referred to say. It will be remembered that October 1, 1886, by invitation of the Clerical Union of Brooklyn, the Secretary of the

New York Society for the Suppression of Vice presented the facts to the ministers of Brooklyn at a meeting held in the hall of the Brooklyn Y. M. C. A. A committee was then and there appointed, at the request of the speaker, consisting of the following gentlemen, to investigate as to the truthfulness of statements then made, to wit : Revs. George E. Reed, Thomas A. Nelson, Jesse B. Thomas, Alfred J. Hutton, I. J. Lansing, J. C. Ager, Edward B. Terhune, Justin D. Fulton, George F. Pentecost, and Lindsay Parker, to whom additions afterwards were made as follows : L. T. Chamberlain, Rabbi William Sparger, G. F. Behringer, W. H. Thomas, Father Malone, A. J. Canfield, and John W. Chadwick.

This committee made a thorough examination into the statements, records of the courts, and into the law. They invited Messrs. Ridgway and Catlin and heard what they had to say in their own defence, and then concluded their report as follows :

" 1. In conclusion the committee beg to say that after patient and laborious examination of the facts within their reach, together with the statements of interested parties, *they do not find that Mr. Comstock's statements can be successfully impeached in any essential particular.*

" 2. That the provisions of the law, and the resources for its enforcement within reach of the District Attorney, during the past nine years, have been ample for the suppression of the evils complained of, as is evidenced by the statements of the present District Attorney concerning its recent—and, as he alleges, complete—extinction, as well as from the facts and other data herewith submitted, and *that the persistent and public continuance of gambling in Kings County during that period argues most reprehensible delinquency on the part of the persons implicated in these charges.*"

Mr. Ridgway had the brazen effrontery, February 5, 1887, when before Governor Hill, arguing his motion to dismiss our charges, to say : "The clergymen vindicated me, and some of them went the next Sunday and preached in

my favor, while others denounced the gentlemen opposing
me." The committee also say :

" 3. That while the primary responsibility for failure to enforce existing
laws against gaming rests with the District Attorney, the facts, nevertheless, which have come before the committee force them to the conviction that among officials at large, concerned in the administration of
the law under consideration, there has been exhibited a failure to realize
the gravity and extent of the gambling evil and an inexcusable lethargy
in its suppression."

The report was unanimously adopted by the gentlemen
present, including a large number of clergy and others who
had gathered to hear the report of this committee.

This report was submitted October 29, 1886.

Reader, who is telling the truth ?

,

CHAPTER VII.

MORE OUTRAGES AGAINST LAW AND JUSTICE.

Go back now to September, 1884, and we can find evidence to confirm James E. Kelly, the boss gambler, when he said, June 30, in prophetic words of consolation, to his trembling associates in crime : "The Grand Jury will adjourn and the indictments will be pigeon-holed, etc. At any rate, our business will not be interfered with this season."

Was there a contract to protect these gamblers? I do not say. Contract or no contract, they were protected from prosecution, despite our best efforts, and their unlawful business was not interfered with, even though good evidence was secured against them, and placed at the disposal of the District Attorney.

The Fall season on the Sheepshead Bay race course opened in September, 1884. The same gamblers who had been indicted the June before again appeared with their gambling paraphernalia and occupied the fifty or more booths.

No sooner had gambling commenced than many rumors began to circulate, and boasts of gamblers that they were all right ; that they " had everybody fixed " ; that there would be no interference allowed throughout the season ; even the New York Society for the Suppression of Vice had been silenced and would do nothing.

On or about the 10th day of September, 1884, the follow-ing came in a letter to our office, charging that an employé of Mr. Kelly had secured my silence and controlled me by the payment of $2500.

Mr. ANTHONY COMSTOCK,

Dear Sir :—

I have been disappointed that your Society has taken no action this fall towards the suppression of pool-selling on the race grounds at Coney Island. I watched your efforts last spring with a great deal of pride, and although through the apathy of the officials in Kings County, whose duty it was to aid you, you failed to suppress it, still persistent effort on your part will banish the glaring evil as effectually as your efforts have ridden the community of the pest of vicious literature. I write you now particularly for your own vindication. I have been told that a man connected with the Coney Island Jockey Club, named Roe or Rowe, has said that he had secured your silence and controlled you by the payment of $2500. I believe this to be false, but notorious gamblers, including Michael Murray and James Kelly, have openly boasted in the Fifth Avenue Hotel that this was accomplished.

We do not lie under any such charges or insinuations without doing something to vindicate ourselves. Immediately upon the receipt of this letter steps were taken to nail this lie. Two things were done.

First, the following advertisement was inserted in the Brooklyn papers, to wit :

BLACKMAILER ADVERTISED.

" Within the last few days rumors have come to me that certain parties are demanding and receiving blackmail from pool-sellers and gamblers in the County of Kings in my name. Again, it is reported that a man named Roe, or Rowe, has given it out that he has paid me $2500. In view of the above statements, which are each and every one of them maliciously false, so far as I am concerned, I desire, through your columns, to offer a reward of $50, for evidence sufficient to convict any person guilty of blackmailing any gambler, or any other person, in my name or the name of the New York Society for the Suppression of Vice.

" Also for evidence that will sustain a suit for slander against any person who says or represents that he or any other person has so unlawfully paid money to me or any agent of this Society. Any representation that I have ever, directly or indirectly, received money from a criminal is false *in toto*, and if any other person is receiving or claiming to receive money in my name, I desire to know the fact.

" Respectfully yours,

" ANTHONY COMSTOCK."

A still more effectual measure was adopted, but failed, through no fault of ours, as the facts will show.

Secondly, September 16 we secured the positive evidence against *seventeen* gamblers, *thirteen* of whom were of those who had been indicted, protected, and shielded from arrest or interference with their unlawful business the June previous.

Complaints were drawn in due form of law, and September 18 these complaints, with the witnesses, were taken to Mr. Ridgway's office. He was not to be found.

The following letter was left in his office on the same date. This letter contains the names of the defendant gamblers, the names of the witnesses, and the specific crime charged.

Read this letter carefully, and then say whether or no Mr. Ridgway " had reason to believe these gamblers offenders against Chapter IX. of the Penal Code," particularly Section 351.

FIRST LETTER TO MR. RIDGWAY, OF SEPTEMBER 18, 1884.

THE NEW YORK SOCIETY FOR THE SUPPRESSION OF VICE, 150 NASSAU STREET, ROOM 9.

NEW YORK, *Sept.* 16, 1884.

Hon. JAMES A. RIDGWAY,
District Attorney County of Kings,
Brooklyn, N. Y.

Sir :—

I respectfully call attention to the fact that I have positive evidence that at Sheepshead Bay race track the following parties, who were indicted in June, are continuing in the most open and positive manner to violate the laws of this State, particularly Section 351 of the Penal Code, to wit: James E. Kelly, Daniel Gleason, John S. Stow, Albert H. Cridge, William Warring, William McNamara, James Dunn, Michael

Murray, Daniel Wartzfelder, James Varley, David J. Johnson, F. K. Bradley and T. J. Meehan.

In addition to the above, the following parties were also present violating the law, to wit: Edward Ross, William Lovell, John Clark, and John Doe, the last two whose real names are unknown, but who can be identified.

I beg also to present further, that on the 16th day of September Messrs. Joseph A. Britton, George E. Oram, and Elias C. Baldwin, of this office, were sent by me to investigate and see if the laws were violated at Sheepshead Bay race track, and each of them is waiting in this office with affidavits drawn certifying to the open and flagrant violation of the law by the above named parties in their presence on that day, ready to go, if you will permit or direct, to your assistants in Brooklyn, and with your assistant before any Supreme Court Judge or County Judge, and secure warrants and search warrants for the arrest of these gamblers and the seizure of the unlawful paraphernalia exposed and there being used by them.

The urgency of this case lies in the fact that to-day, to-morrow, and next day the races continue, and these men will continue their unlawful business.

Please take notice that I have the affidavits drawn and signed by the complaining witnesses, and that I have been over to Brooklyn to see you personally in reference to this matter, and am informed by the assistants in your office that you are in attendance in court in New York as a witness. I therefore write these facts and respectfully ask that you will give such direction in this matter as will enable us to secure warrants for the arrest of these men, and search warrants to seize their unlawful paraphernalia thus being publicly used and employed in violation of the law of this State, in order that we may arrest these parties this afternoon while they continue to violate the law.

I have the honor to be,

Very respectfully yours, etc.,

(Signed) ANTHONY COMSTOCK,

Sec'y N. Y. Soc. for the S. of V.

Not hearing from Mr. Ridgway, another letter was sent the same day, asking him to telegraph us what hour the next morning we could see him.

The witnesses were also sent over, and remained at his office until after three o'clock P. M.   He came not.

Sept. 18, 1884.

Hon. JAMES W. RIDGWAY,
   District Attorney County of Kings,
      Brooklyn, N. Y.

Sir :—

This morning about half-past ten I called at your office, and was informed you had gone to the General Sessions Court in New York. I wrote a letter and sent it over to you there; 'but found you had gone from there. I then returned with the witnesses to Brooklyn in hopes of finding you, and left the witnesses with instructions to remain and see you up to and until after three o'clock. They report that they were unable to see you.

I therefore take the liberty of sending herewith to you this letter to further ask that you will telegraph me in the morning what hour I can see you at your office to-morrow morning.

I will have the witnesses there to prove that all of the persons named in my letter of to-day, which I left at your office, were on the 16th inst. openly violating the laws of the State, and there is every reason to believe will continue to do so, so long as the races last at Sheepshead Bay.

As there are but two days' more races on the programme for this month, I especially ask that you will allow me to bring the affidavits, which are already signed by the witnesses, and have them submitted to one of the judges of the County Court, or Supreme Court Judge, in order that warrants may be issued to arrest the men openly defying the laws of this State, and to seize paraphernalia that has been used publicly and openly during two months of the present year at least, to wit : June and September.

I beg to say that, inasmuch as you informed me that you had men employed at Brighton Beach race course at Coney Island to secure the evidence against the gamblers there, I have turned my attention more directly to the Sheepshead Bay race track, so as not to have any conflict with your officers.

I am informed that some of the men that were indicted last October have been in the business at Brighton Beach during the entire summer, and if your men cannot find these men thus openly violating the law, if you will send them to me I will be very happy to inform them where these men are doing business openly—so openly, indeed, that they will only have to pass by on the public thoroughfare to see the open violation of law.

' I would also respectfully submit that if you would subpœna Chief of Police McKane, he would be able doubtless to give you important evidence, as a large gambling establishment has been open for the sale of pools nearly opposite to his headquarters during the entire season.

Very respectfully yours,

(Signed) ANTHONY COMSTOCK,

Secretary.

Mr. Ridgway, in his answer to the Governor, swears he had no information that any of the men continued to violate the laws.

Hearing nothing from Mr. Ridgway, the next day, Sept. 19, 1884, the writer and witnesses again went over to Brooklyn, to the District Attorney's office. He had gone to New York. We were informed that a letter had been sent to our office by Mr. Ridgway. We returned and found the following :

LETTER FROM MR. RIDGWAY, DATED SEPT. 19, 1884.

OFFICE OF THE DISTRICT ATTORNEY, KINGS COUNTY.

COURT HOUSE, ROOM 3, BROOKLYN, N. Y.

Sept. 19, 1884.

Mr. A. COMSTOCK,

Dear Sir :—

I am in receipt of your communication of the 18th inst. calling my attention to certain violations of Section 351, of the Penal Code, on the 16 inst., and informing me that Joseph A. Britton, George E. Oram, and Elias C. Baldwin were present and witnessed such violations, and that they are prepared to furnish proof as to the fact of such violations. You are hereby notified to produce the above named witnesses before one of the Justices of the Peace of the town in which such violations took place, at one o'clock this day, at the Town Hall in the town of Gravesend, at which time assistant District Attorney Clark will be present, prepared to act for the prosecution and to render all the assistance necessary to prepare the complaints and obtain the warrants necessary for the arrest of the parties against whom the proof is furnished.

Very respectfully yours,

(Signed) JAS. W. RIDGWAY.

This letter was received by us too late for us to have reached Coney Island in time, even if we had been duly subpœnaed to go there. *We were not subpœnaed at all.*

Immediately upon the receipt of this letter we made answer by writing the following letter, which was received and read by Mr. Ridgway, in presence of the writer and one of our assistants, the same day. Mr. Ridgway was at the General Sessions Court House, in New York City, in the Hall adjoining Part II., when he received and read it.

This letter states why we would not voluntarily go before a Justice of the Peace of the town of Gravesend. We submit that our reasons are cogent and wise.

Before reading this letter, note what Mr. Ridgway *swears* to, in his answer to our charges before the Governor, concerning the reasons why we did not go before the Justices at Gravesend. Take his oath and compare it with our documentary evidence, and then where is he? He swears as though there was no other ground of our objection to go to Gravesend. He says:—

"That said Comstock on that day, in answer to respondent's request, wrote to respondent a letter in which he refused to appear before a Justice of the Peace of the town of Gravesend, and alleged as a reason for such refusal that he and his officers were in fear of some personal violence, yet, notwithstanding such declination, the officers whom he referred to were actually upon the race track on that day, and were engaged in the buying of pools."

The witnesses were all in our office in New York City awaiting Mr. Ridgway's orders, and four witnesses can prove this, notwithstanding Mr. Ridgway's oath. He swears positively; as from personal knowledge. Now read the evidence against Mr. Ridgway's oath.

LETTER TO JAMES W. RIDGWAY, SEPT. 19, 1884.

NEW YORK, *Sept.* 19, 1884.

Hon. JAMES W. RIDGWAY,
    District Attorney County of Kings,
        Brooklyn, N. Y.

Dear Sir:—

I am in receipt of your favor of the 19th inst., notifying me that you have received mine, and also notifying me to produce the witnesses before one of the Justices of the Peace of the town of Gravesend at one o'clock to-day, at which time assistant District Attorney Clark will be present prepared to act for the prosecution, etc.

In reply I respectfully present to you, the same as I have presented before, that I do not consider the Justices of the Peace of the town of Gravesend proper persons to present these cases before.

First, because I understand and am informed that they are by law the Commissioners of Police, and as such Commissioners have authority and control over the police of that town, and having such control, have allowed their subordinates to be present throughout the season where these laws have been violated, protecting the gamblers' interest.

If they are not Police Commissioners, then I am wrongly advised in reference to the matter and should be glad to be advised by you. If they are Police Commissioners and have allowed their subordinates year after year, as has been the case, to stand where the laws are openly violated, and to aid and abet these men by preserving order while the gamblers violate the law, then they are not proper persons to administer the law against the gamblers whose interest they have protected.

Second, as was fully stated to you in June last; there is no adequate police protection for the agents of this Society to protect them from the violence of the mob of gamblers and cut-throats that congregate in these places, and I will not consent that the lives of the agents of this Society shall be jeopardized, when the law permits and makes it equally the duty of any Supreme Court Judge or County Judge to whom application is made on behalf of the people to issue their warrants and apprehend these men.

Another reason for making the request that you take the matter before the County Judges or Supreme Judge is, that to arrest seventeen of these gamblers and seize the unlawful paraphernalia which these men there have in public use, requires a larger force than the police force of the town of Gravesend can furnish independent of the police officers who are paid by those interested in the conducting of these gambling schemes, and who are constantly in attendance upon these crimes.

It is well known to you that the sheriff's officers have already been assaulted by the local police.

It is equally well known to you that the crimes of which I complain are so openly conducted that every official in the County of Kings is aware of the fact, and especially the police of Gravesend, who knowingly permit these laws to be violated, and I respectfully submit that as District Attorney of the County of Kings, with a full knowledge of these facts, you have no right to expect three or four men to go down and face the mob of gamblers and outlaws far away from police protection, with local officials angered because of what they call our interference, when we as citizens obtain the evidence of crime and bring it to your office and ask for the enforcement of these laws.

I place the responsibility upon you of bringing these men to justice, now, while they are openly violating the law. The complaints are drawn and signed by the witnesses and ready to be taken before any one of the County Judges or Supreme Court Judges in the city of Brooklyn.

We are ready to go at a moment's notice before any of those judges; but as for sending my men down to face this mob of law-breakers, it shall not be done with my consent, because I know that it is placing the lives of these men in jeopardy. And if one of them should lose his life, I should feel that I was guilty of murder in yielding to the demand which you thus make upon me, with a full knowledge of the facts before you.

These are unusual crimes that are being committed.

During the month of June, as you well know, and again during the month of September, with your knowledge and consent, these gamblers have openly defied the law, and you have failed to bring them to justice, to put one of them on trial, or to interfere or permit the unlawful paraphernalia which they use for gambling to be in any manner seized or disturbed. And I don't propose that you, as District Attorney, shall shirk the responsibility by any such subterfuge as that set out in your letter of the 19th inst.

When the gamblers defied the law in the County of Queens, and the local authorities would not act, Justice Gilbert, of the Supreme Court, mindful of the obligations of his office, promptly issued his warrants, and these men were arrested.

Repeatedly in the courts in the County of New York the judges of the higher courts, when applied to, have issued their warrants, and the men have been arrested.

Now, sir, again I present to you these affidavits and witnesses, and demand in the name of the laws which you have knowingly permitted to be outraged the arrest of the criminals whom you have knowingly permitted to violate the law even after they were indicted.

I call upon you, in the name of the people of the State of New York, to take these papers and witnesses before some judge who is not in any way beholden to these men, and where the witnesses shall be protected in their lives and liberty, and bring these men to justice. If this cannot be done, then I respectfully demand of you that the witnesses be brought at once before the Grand Jury and immediate action be taken.

You will pardon any show of feeling in this letter, but it comes from an earnest determination to see laws that have been year after year in the most public manner outraged and violated, respected, enforced, and obeyed.

You, as District Attorney, knowingly permit professional gamblers to come within the jurisdiction of your courts and continue their nefarious business without let or hindrance on your part, while the indictments filed by the Grand Jury in your county slumber in your office I am ready to co-operate to the fullest extent in any reasonable and proper manner to secure the enforcement of these laws, and that at once, and I demand at your hands prompt and immediate action, that these laws may be enforced against this organized band of criminals.

I have the honor to be, sir,

Very respectfully yours, etc.,

(Signed) ANTHONY COMSTOCK,

Secretary.

After Mr. Ridgway had read this letter he turned and said to the writer : " I notify you in the presence of this witness that I have sent Mr. Clark down to the Town Hall of Gravesend, and have arranged to have a magistrate there, and I sent you word to take your witnesses and go there, and that Mr. Clark was there to attend to the matter." To which the writer replied : " Yes, I admit receiving a letter embodying in substance what you have said, but in return I notify you that I went over this whole matter last June, and showed you that the Justices of the Peace are by law Police Commissioners ; that they appointed the policemen at Gravesend, permitted them to be employed by the gamblers, and detailed them to witness the daily violations of law, the gamblers and those interested in the races paying their weekly salaries. I am informed by one of the Justices of Peace that they are, by law, Police Commissioners, and that they have appointed these men as special policemen, sworn them in as policemen and then assigned them to the gamblers, and that the gamblers pay them as policemen. This is an extraordinary crime, where these men have for years openly defied the laws, and where the local officials knowingly permit these laws to be violated; and I say to you that as for sending the matter before such creatures as these, who, while holding offices of Justices of the Peace, are also Police Commissioners, and as such appoint men to protect these gamblers, and then on the other hand attempt to administer the law against the criminals whom they appoint men to assist, I will not be party to any such outrage.

" It must be apparent to you that such creatures are not qualified to administer justice against those whom they are thus protecting while these laws are openly violated, and were violated during the month of June, as you know, and have been violated during the month of September, and you know it ; and you know that the business is so openly conducted and the laws so openly violated that you cannot walk by there without seeing it. The paraphernalia there now is the same which was used in June, which you then would not allow to be seized, and I called your attention to the Code where it says, ' It is the duty of the officials to seize it.' "

I also said further :—

" It is reported that the reason that these men are not brought to trial is because they have paid large amounts of money. It is further charged that they have paid $2500 a month at Brighton Beach and $18,000 at Sheepshead Bay, for this fall season, not to be interfered with. I have secured the evidence and have the affidavits drawn, and bring the responsibility to you as prosecuting attorney and place it at your door."

"Well," he said, " I propose to do my duty."

We then made a formal demand upon Mr. Ridgway to have the cases brought before the Grand Jury, or that he should send one of his assistants with me before any reputable judge in Kings County who had the authority and jurisdiction in these cases.

I told Mr. Ridgway that I would hold the witnesses at my office subject to his orders, and did so keep them there all that day, Mr. Ridgway's oath to the contrary notwithstanding.

REASONS WHY WE WOULD NOT GO TO LOCAL AUTHORITIES OF GRAVESEND.

Aside from reasons already given, John Y. McKane and eight of his subordinates were under indictment upon our complaints for aiding gamblers and violating Sec. 349, Penal Code.

They were hostile to us and friendly to the gamblers.

McKane had brazenly defied law, oath of office, and public sentiment by his public announcements, if what the papers said was true, as to what he would and would not do concerning gambling on the race courses at Gravesend.

April 22, 1884, in an interview had with John Y. McKane, published in the New York *World*, the following occurs :

"What will you do about pool-selling on the race tracks ?"

McKane—" I don't propose to interfere with the pool-selling at Brighton Beach or Sheepshead Bay."

The Brooklyn *Union* of the same date prints an interview with Mr. McKane as follows :

Reporter—" Well, don't you suppose they will have pool-selling on the race tracks ?   What will you do with them ? "

McKane—" I don't propose to interfere with Brighton Beach or the Jockey Club at Sheepshead Bay."

These statements have never been denied, so far as I can learn.

The following is what the Bacon Investigating committee said of and recommended concerning Mr. John Y. McKane:

" He himself testified that one man detailed by him to stop public pool-selling on a race track might do it. The mere presence of the Sheriff on the Brighton Beach track stopped the gambling there completely for the day of his visit and for the next three racing days. As to this form of gambling Mr. McKane stated to us his position even more emphatically than he had done as to the gross and vile offences perpetrated on Coney Island. He held that no certainty on his part that the law was being violated required him, Chief of Police though he was, to interfere to maintain the law; that he should refuse to put the machinery of the law in motion or to move himself, unless upon specific and formal complaints brought to him and pressed upon him, and that even when he visited the places where the law was being violated he should carefully refrain from any general interference with the violation of the law which was taking place before his very eyes, and should merely arrest the particular persons against whom he had formal complaints. Such has been and is Mr. McKane's position, in spite of the explicit command of the law, of which he was a sworn and responsible officer. Mr. McKane's conduct has been that of an enemy, and not a friend, of the administration of justice. He has flagrantly and intentionally violated the law. Whatever may have been his motive, this conduct should lead in his prompt prosecution and removal from office. It is impossible, however, to resist the conclusion that for his open, prolonged and loyal assent to the continuance of these criminal practices, there was some direct motive to a person of Mr McKane's ability, vigor, industry and thrift. It was proved that these practices brought to those engaged in them an enormous money revenue. Mr. McKane admitted that he received from them large sums of money, which he says, indeed, were for work done by him as a builder, partly, as will be remembered, in constructing the very apparatus necessary to the perpetration of crime. But surely a chief of police who assents to the commission of crime, after he has received money from those who practise it, can hardly complain if the public decline to be content with his bare statement that his employment to do work and his receipt of money had no relation to the indulgence and the immunity which he extended to those from whom he received the money.

" The committee recommends the immediate indictment and the prompt

8

prosecution of John Y. McKane, in order that, if convicted, he may not only be punished, but be removed from the offices whose trust he has so completely betrayed.

The following is a list of offices filled in Gravesend by Messrs. McKane, Waring & Co.

TOWN OF GRAVESEND.

Member of Assembly.
R. V. B. NEWTON, D.

TOWN OFFICIALS.
Supervisor.
JOHN Y. McKANE, D.*

Justices of the Peace.
JACQUES S. STRYKER, R.
ANTHONY WARING, D.
JOHN McMAHON, D.
R. V. B. NEWTON, D.

Board of Police Commissioners.
JOHN Y. McKANE, Supervisor, D.
JACQUES S. STRYKER, Justice of the Peace, R.
ANTHONY WARING,   "   "   "   D.
JOHN McMAHON,   "   "   "   D.
R. V. B. NEWTON,   "   "   "   D.

Board of Health.
JOHN Y. McKANE, Supervisor, D.
JACQUES S. STRYKER, Justice of the Peace, R.
ANTHONY WARING,   "   "   "   D.

---

* Superintendent Sunday School M. E. Church.

JOHN McMAHON,   Justice of the Peace, D.
R. V. B. NEWTON,   "   "   "   D.
S. STRYKER WILLIAMSON, Citizen Member, D.
JOHN L. VOORHIES, Town Clerk, D.

Town Board.

JOHN Y. McKANE, Supervisor, D.
JACQUES S. STRYKER, Justice of the Peace, R.
ANTHONY WARING,   "   "   "   D.
JOHN McMAHON,   "   "   "   D.
R. V. B. NEWTON,   "   "   "   D.
JOHN L. VOORHIES, Town Clerk, D.

Board of Town Auditors.

JOHN Y. McKANE, Supervisor, D.
JACQUES S. STRYKER, Justice of the Peace, R.
ANTHONY WARING,   "   "   "   D.
JOHN McMAHON,   "   "   "   D.
R. V. B. NEWTON,   "   "   "   D.
JOHN L. VOORHIES, Town Clerk, D.
Or any two of the said Justices of the Peace (see Chap.
305, Laws 1840, Sec. 1).

Chairman, pro tem., Board of Supervisors, Kings County.

JOHN Y. McKANE, D.

Who appoints all the Committees of the Board, by virtue
of his office.

D.—Democrat.
R.—Republican.

That the public may be advised of the character of some
of the men whose duty it was to enforce the laws against
gambling, and before whom, as Justices of the Peace, we
were expected to appear, I present extracts from the printed

reports of the testimony of Anthony Warring, Justice of the
Peace and Police Commissioner of Gravesend, as given before the Bacon Investigating Committee, as follows :

By Mr. W. W. Goodrich—

Q. Do you consider it a part of your duty, as a member of
the Police Department, to sit until somebody comes and
makes a complaint before you ?

A. Yes, sir.

Q. And you never take any steps ?

A. I never take any steps to look up crime.

Q. And you mean to convey the impression that you could
be on a race track often, weekly, for three years, and never
know that gambling was going on ?

A. Yes, sir.

Q. And you swear that was a fact ?

A. Yes, sir.

Q. With your knowledge and experience on race courses
you had no reason to believe, you saw nothing which indi-
cated to your mind, that gambling was going on on these
race courses ?

A. I did not, sir.

Mr. Goodrich sat down, disgusted with the effrontery of
this swearing official.   Whereupon Mr. Parsons, the senior
counsel, took him in hand.

By Mr. Parsons : Q. I wish to satisfy my curiosity on one
point.   Do you know what a booth is ?

A. I do not, sir.

Q. Mr. Warring, we will begin at the beginning.   Did you
ever hear the term " pool," or " pool-selling," or see it in the
newspapers ?

A. I can't say positively; I may have seen it—I can't say
positively.   I have heard a great deal of it since this investigation began.

Q. Prior to this investigation did you ever see it in print
or hear the expression ?

A. I might have seen or heard it.

Q. Is that the strongest statement you can make upon that—you might have seen or heard it?

A. It is.

Q. Have you any idea of the meaning of pool-selling?

A. I have not.

Q. Do you know whether it has anything to do with a Sunday-school, a public school, or a church, or the meeting of the Board of Aldermen, or proceedings in a court, or what?

A. I don't know anything about it.

Q. Does it not associate itself in your mind with anything else?

A. No, sir.

Q. Mr. Warring, do you appreciate that this testimony which you are giving is under oath?

A. I do, certainly.

This lying wretch then thought he was through, and was about to leave the stand, when Mr. Goodrich again turned the crank, and the following swearing to order appeared:

Q. Did you have any business connection with either of the race tracks at any time in 1882 or 1883?

A. In 1882 I was on the race tracks.

Q. Which race track were you on?

A. On the Brighton.

Q. What position did you hold in connection with that club?

A. I was cashier.

Q. How long were you there?

A. 1881 and 1882.

Q. And you still mean to give the impression that, although you were four months cashier of a restaurant under the Grand Stand of the race track in 1882, you do not know what pool-selling is?

A. I do not know what pool-selling is.

At the next session of the Committee Warring brought in his docket as a Justice of the Peace. It contained eighteen cases against persons who had been arrested during his term of Justice, from 1883 to present date, for violation of gambling laws. Every case but one had been "discharged," "John Y. McKane, complainant." One case was docketed, "Gambling, arraigned and settled."

One out of the entire number pleaded "guilty," and sentence was suspended. Not one was held for the action of the Grand Jury.

Mr. Parsons again put in the probe. Turning to page 81 of Warring's docket, to the case of "People *vs.* John Matthews," and showing it to Warring, he said:

Q. The question is whose hand-writing it is.

A. It is my hand-writing.

Q. Is all the entry in your hand-writing?

A. I think every entry in it is my hand-writing, sir.

Q. What, in that entry, have you stated as the offence for which he was brought before you?

A. Stated as "selling pools"; that is the charge.

And so they went through the docket, showing case after case where the same or similar entry was made by him. Then the counsel took up some of the complaints, also drawn by Warring, in his own hand-writing, and handing the same to this brazen creature, had him read the charge for like offences.

Then these unmerciful inquirers kept at this elastic swearer until they proved from his own lips that he had actually purchased pools himself. They also drew out the interesting fact that the very day he was first subpœnaed to appear before the Committee he spent the afternoon with Battersby, Engeman & Co., at the Brighton Beach race course, Clifton, N. J., while racing and pool-selling were going on.

Subsequently witnesses appeared before the Committee and swore positively to seeing Warring, while Justice of the Peace and Police Commissioner, hob-nobbing with gamblers and purchasing pools, etc.

In the official report, adopted by the assembly, May 10, 1887, we find these words :

" Mr? McKane's four associates upon the Police Board and the other four boards of Gravesend deserve severe censure for their acquiescence in the course taken by their chief. To only one of them is it, however, practicable to here specially refer. Anthony Waring is a justice of the peace, having his office on Coney Island itself, and as such he is the most important magistrate in a neighborhood in which criminal practices are so prevalent and so offensive and dangerous to the multitudes seeking health and recreation at the seashore. He is one of the Board of Police, but when asked as to his performance of official duty he testified, " I never take any steps to look up crime." This testimony needs, however, to be qualified. Mr. Waring could perhaps have said with truth that he never looked up crime to punish it; but that he looked up crime to engage in it was abundantly proved. He himself participated in the criminal practices to which we have referred and which it was his sworn and special duty to punish. And in the immediate presence of this committee Mr. Waring committed what we believe to be a serious offence, for which he should be punished. He testified in a variety of forms, and after being cautioned as to the significance of what he was saying, that he had no idea of the meaning of pool-selling ; that pool-selling did not associate itself in his mind with anything else ; that he did not know what pool-selling was. He admitted that in 1882, after being a schoolteacher, he was cashier at a restaurant directly under the grand stand on the Brighton Beach racing track, where, as was proved, pool-selling was openly and notoriously carried on to an enormous extent. It appeared that Mr. Waring has since been active in the affairs of Gravesend, among whose most conspicuous features have been its racing tracks and the pool-selling and gambling there carried on ; that as a police commissioner and justice of the peace he has had exceptionally good means of information ; that before him as justice of the peace, John Y. McKane prosecuted in September and October, 1883, three different defendants, Matthews, Crosby and Miller, all for " selling pools," the cases being at last dismissed because the prosecutor did not appear in either case, and the entries, including the description of the charge, all being in Mr. Waring's handwriting; that he had read Section 351 of the Penal Code with reference to pool-selling; that when he was subpœnaed as a witness he was on his way to Clifton, N. J., a race track of Messrs. A. H. Battersby and George H. Engeman, two of the proprietors of the Brighton Beach racing track, gentlemen both of whom are under indictment for pool-selling, and that at their race track at Clifton he had himself bought in a pool. Mr. Waring's position as a Police Commissioner and as the Justice of the Peace at Coney Island made material to our inquiry, as he perfectly well knew, his knowledge of pool-selling. To shield himself from a charge of official dereliction he swore repeatedly to entire ignorance of a matter of which he was proved to have actual knowledge and the amplest means of knowledge. In our opinion he committed deliberate, wilful perjury. Doubtless other witnesses before us, beside Mr. Waring, saw fit to testify to an ignorance of matters which no one doubts they must have known. But this case of a judicial and executive officer is peculiarly flagrant. It will be a disgraceful failure of justice at the very fountain seat of justice if Mr. Waring be longer permitted to hold his offices in Gravesend. We recommend to the Grand Jury of Kings County an examination of the facts to which we have referred and which are easy to prove; and, if the facts be as we have learned them to be, we recommend the immediate indictment and vigorous prosecution of Mr. Waring for perjury, and to the Supreme Court a proper proceeding to remove him from his office of justice of the peace."

This is one of the authorities of Gravesend to whom it was expected, in the natural order of events, we were to apply to enforce the laws against gamblers.

What is the difference between an official who swears to discharge a certain duty, and does not do it, and a witness who swears upon the witness stand to tell the truth, the whole truth, and nothing but the truth, and does not do it? Are not both morally guilty of perjury? Should not such a crime receive the execration of every honest person?

What! apply to a man to arrest himself or seize his own interests! Bah!

Turning now to the cases in hand, *Mr. Ridgway has never subpœnaed a single one of these witnesses before any Court, Grand Jury, or Magistrate,* nor has he taken any steps, so far as we can ascertain, to bring these men to justice in any manner or form on these complaints. It was not until July

16, 1886, nearly two years afterwards, when an appeal was made directly to the Grand Jury by a letter to the foreman, that we could get these cases into court at all. Then it was that the writer demanded of the Grand Jury the indictment of James W. Ridgway for violation of Section 349 of the Penal Code, in not "informing against and prosecuting" these defendants. This resulted in the indictment of the *seventeen* gamblers against whom evidence was secured in September, 1884, these being the cases referred to in the letters of September 18 and 19, 1884, to Mr. Ridgway.

The letter to the Grand Jury was as follows, and I present it in this connection because it is a part of this history. It shows our fidelity, and answers gross misstatements made concerning it by Mr. Ridgway in his remarkable answer to the charges preferred against him to the Governor of the State, referred to above.

OFFICE OF THE NEW YORK SOCIETY FOR THE SUP-
PRESSION OF VICE, NO. 150 NASSAU ST.

NEW YORK, *July* 16, 1886.
Mr. HENRY F. VAN LOVAN,
 Foreman of the Grand Jury,
  Brooklyn, N. Y.

Dear Sir :—

I beg to call the attention of the Grand Jury to the fact that the laws against pool gambling, in Kings County, are constantly being violated; that during the past three years men continue to keep public places on the Sheepshead Bay race track and on the race track of the Brighton Beach Association, with paraphernalia for recording bets and wagers, and continue to record bets and wagers, in violation of the law, all action of the court to the contrary.

That last month agents of this Society went to the race tracks and procured evidence against Samuel Emery and two of his assistants, and a report was made to the District Attorney. I have this day sent him a full and detailed account of the transaction, with the names of the witnesses, and I respectfully ask that this matter may be brought before the Grand Jury, and these men indicted.

I beg to present, for the information of the Grand Jury, that during the months of June and September of each year, at Sheepshead Bay race track, the laws are openly violated. In 1884 the Grand Jury, in June, found indictments against twenty-two gamblers. Among them were such notorious gamblers as James E. Kelly, Michael Murray, David J. Johnson, Albert H. Cridge, John McDougall, Daniel Gleason, John S. Stow, William Warring, William McNamara, Daniel Wartzfelder, James Varley, F. K. Bradley, and T. J. Meehan. None of these men were arrested until after the indictments were found by the Grand Jury, and none of them were allowed to be arrested, but the bench warrants that were issued remained unexecuted, while the officers from the District Attorney's office went to the gamblers' booths, while they were actually violating the law, and instead of arresting the men that the bench warrants called for, notified them, while they were actually violating the law, to appear the next morning (at a time when it would not interfere with their unlawful business) and give bail. And this, I am informed, was done by order of the District Attorney of Kings County.

The June season closed on the 1st of July. The men gave bail in the morning and returned to their unlawful business in the afternoon. The indictments were filed on June 30, but before these indictments were filed some one, evidently, had informed the gamblers, as the following persons were awaiting to give bail, and did give bail, on the 30th of June, 1884, to wit: Michael Murray, John McDougall, James E. Kelly, Thomas Murray, John S. Stow, Herman Snyder, Mark Jordan, James Dunn, David J. Johnson, and Albert H. Cridge. Officers were sent down with the bench warrants to arrest the other parties, who did not appear in the morning, and found the persons who had given bail in the morning, with the other parties, in their booths openly violating the law

In September, 1884, the persons first named in this letter were found openly violating the same law for which they had been indicted. Complaints were made and presented to the District Attorney of Kings County, by myself in person, with the names of the witnesses and the positive evidence of the guilt of these men, and not one of those witnesses has ever been called or examined by any Grand Jury.

In June, 1885, the same set of gamblers again appeared in the same places at Sheepshead Bay. Again the agents of this Society procured the evidence, and Michael Murray was indicted and arrested. The business continued right on, and has continued on, from that time down to the present time, during each season of June and September, 1885, and June, 1886, and yet Murray has not been tried.

Michael Murray was convicted in New York City in 1884 for a similar offence ; indeed, he was in court in New York in the morning, and he was found violating the same law in Kings County the same afternoon, and upon this evidence was indicted. Upon his demurrer a judgment of conviction was entered upon this indictment, and an appeal was taken by him to the General Term of the Supreme Court. The General Term in May, 1885, affirmed the judgment of conviction. That order of affirmance was entered in the County Clerk's office, June 8, 1885, against Michael Murray and the following other gamblers ; to wit : James E. Kelly, John S. Stow, Thomas Murray, John Kelly, John McDougall, alias Dougal McDougall, David J. Johnson, Albert H. Cridge, Martin Jordan, and James Dunn. Notwithstanding this unanimous affirmance of judgment of conviction in the above cases, neither of these cases has been sentenced, nor has there been, so far as I have been able to find, from a personal examination made a few weeks ago in the office of the Clerk of the Court of Appeals, any appeal perfected in this case.

Michael Murray has not been tried upon the indictment found subsequently to the affirmance by the Supreme Court. This gambling has been permitted to go right on without interruption. Officers who go there with warrants do not seize the paraphernalia. Gamblers are notified as soon as the officers who have the warrants leave the track, and they then open up their business and carry it on.

Last year men were sworn in as special policemen and deputy sheriffs, and in the garb of a "peace officer" guarded these gamblers while the law was openly violated by preserving the peace for them. If the daily papers are to be believed, the Brighton Beach races are running constantly while the law is being violated. Men who have been indicted and convicted are unsentenced. Men who have been indicted repeatedly are untried, and yet the violations of law go right on openly.

I therefore appeal directly to the Grand Jury, because I am satisfied that it is not the intent or purpose of the District Attorney of Kings County to enforce these laws.

I am informed by rumor that he proposes, in some way or other, to have the Grand Jury indict me. I beg to say that if there are any charges made against me or my officers, we ask to be heard, and that no hostile element be permitted to enter the Grand Jury room against those who have earnestly, faithfully, and truly, year after year, persistently endeavored to secure the proper enforcement of the law against these notorious crimes.

Conscious of our integrity, we confidently appeal to any Grand Inquest to investigate our action and our conduct, and I am frank to say to you that I am ready to go before that body and lay all the facts without reserve before you, in reference to any act committed by myself or my assistants.

These are extraordinary times. Despite all the efforts of good men to enforce these laws, the same are openly violated, while thousands of dollars are going into the hands of unscrupulous gamblers; and the courts, thus far, have been unable to cope with the evil or to suppress it.

Unless the Grand Jury will make some decided effort, there is no prospect for the public but to expect that in September, at the fall meeting of the Coney Island Jockey Club at Sheepshead Bay, the same disgraceful scenes will be re-enacted as were enacted during the month of June by gamblers openly violating the law of this State.

As a law-abiding citizen, as a representative of this organization, as an individual who has earnestly and faithfully endeavored to enforce these laws, I appeal to this Grand Inquest to examine into the facts, and to relieve Kings County from the odium that now is attached to it.

> Very truly yours,
> ANTHONY COMSTOCK,
> Secretary.

Did Mr. Ridgway know of the lawless character of these men ? In addition to the above letters, another letter was sent him in November of the same year which revealed to him the standing of at least six of those of whom he was so tender.

After the matter had been referred to Governor Cleveland, a notice was sent out to the effect that some of these men were to be tried at once.

In order that Mr. Ridgway should have the facts before him that six of those indicted were old offenders, and had previously been convicted and sentenced, the following letter was sent :

LETTER TO MR. RIDGWAY OF NOVEMBER 17, 1884.

Hon. JAMES W. RIDGWAY,
> District Attorney,
> > Brooklyn, N. Y.

Sir :—I respectfully call your attention to the following facts, to wit : James E. Kelly, John S. Stow and Thomas Murray, on the 16th day of

June, each pleaded guilty in the Special Sessions Court, New York City, to violating Section 351 of the Penal Code, and each was sentenced in said court for such offences, the said Kelly being fined $100, and said Stow and Murray each fined $10.

That on the 1st day of October, 1884, Michael Murray, Daniel Wartzfelder, and James Varley each pleaded guilty to complaints charging the same offences as aforesaid in the same court, and the said Murray was fined $100, and each of the other defendants was fined $25.

These offences were committed in the county of New York and were for violating the same statute for which each of the above·named are indicted in the Kings County Court of Sessions and about to be tried, and I certify to these facts in order that you may present the same to the Court, should any of the parties be convicted and arraigned for sentence.

Respectfully yours,

(Signed)   ANTHONY COMSTOCK,

Secretary.

Mr. Ridgway now swears he never knew that any of these gamblers were old offenders.

In this connection it will be of interest to note that, although after waiting nearly two years we secured their indictment in 1886, we have not yet been able to have some of these men apprehended by due process of law upon these last indictments.

Five of those men, who have not yet been arrested, are already under bail upon the June, 1884, indictments, and their bail-bonds could have been called at any instance and they brought into court. Instead, however, notwithstanding a personal appeal made in November, 1886, to both Mr. Ridgway and Sheriff Farley, none of these men have yet been apprehended.

The following letter to Mr. Ridgway was delivered to him personally by Mr. Oram, to wit:

November 8, 1886.

JAMES W. RIDGWAY, Esq.,
District Attorney Kings County,
Brooklyn, N. Y.

Sir :—I beg to call your attention to the fact that the following parties indicted June 23, 1886, and for whom bench warrants are out for their arrest, have not yet been arrested, to wit: Daniel Wartzfelder, James Varley, James Dunn, William Warring, and William McNamara.

These parties are under bonds on previous indictments in the Sessions Court.

Will you kindly have these cases called in court on the other cases, so that the Sheriff can execute the bench warrants?

The following parties also have not been arrested of those indicted July 23, 1886, to wit: Edward Ross, John Clark, John Doe, Solomon Doe, and Horatio Doe. My assistant will go at any time with one of your officers, or with any of the Sheriff's officers who may have these bench warrants, and identify these men if they can be found.

This office will most cheerfully co-operate at any time in securing these men and in bringing these criminals to justice.

Very respectfully yours,

(Signed) ANTHONY COMSTOCK,

Secretary.

The same day Mr. Oram delivered at Sheriff Farley's office the following letter:

November 8, 1886.

CHARLES B. FARLEY, Esq.,

Sheriff Kings County,

Brooklyn, N. Y.

Sir:—I beg to call your attention to the fact that the following parties, indicted July 23, 1886, and for whom I am informed there are bench warrants now in your possession for their arrest, are the same as are now under bail in the Sessions Court on indictments filed June 30, 1884. The offences for which these parties were indicted under the last indictments of July 23, 1886, are for subsequent offences.

The names of the parties not yet arrested are as follows: Daniel Wartzfelder, James Varley, James Dunn, William Warring, and William McNamara.

Edward Ross, John Clark, John Doe, Solomon Doe, and Horatio Doe have not been arrested at all, and whenever it shall be convenient for you to send an officer with the bench warrants for the arrest of these parties to this office, I will be very happy to detail one of my men to go with him to identify the parties to him.

Some of these men reside in the city of New York, and I have no doubt can be found. The men who have given bail, I think you will find their residences given upon the bail-bonds.

Very respectfully yours,

(Signed)   ANTHONY COMSTOCK,

Secretary.

Does not this continued protection of these five prominent gamblers lend force to the consoling words of James F. Kelly of June 30, 1884, that "the Grand Jury will adjourn and these indictments will be pigeon-holed," etc.?

Is not this persistency not to call these gamblers into court, nor to arrest them, on the part of the prosecuting attorney and Sheriff a circumstance which justifies the belief that there was a contract of protection made with the gamblers? If there was no contract, why should these gamblers be protected? If there was a contract, has it not been faithfully carried out on the part of the Kings County officials?

Contract or no contract, are not these facts outrages upon every sentiment of morality, justice, and law?

CHAPTER VIII.

AN APPEAL TO GOVERNOR CLEVELAND.

Now go back in order to have the record concise. Mr. Ridgway had failed to bring the men indicted under their right names July 23, 1884, into court to plead to these second indictments. It will be remembered that the most of them were in court July 8, 1884, to plead to the first indictment, but all but ten remained mute.

Mr. Ridgway would not subpœna any of the witnesses against the (17) *seventeen* gamblers complained of to him in our letter of September 18, 1884, before any Court or Grand Jury. He did not interfere in any manner or form with these public crimes, although the evidence, witnesses, and complaints were all subject to his order.

The eleven demurrers were undecided, and nothing practically had been done to stop these crimes or punish these notorious criminals. Then it was we appealed to the Governor.

It was not until after the Executive Committee of the New York Society for the Suppression of Vice had in November, 1884, made a written report to Governor Cleveland, calling attention to these facts, and a demand was made that action should be taken against Mr. Ridgway for the non-enforcement of law, that definite action was taken in these cases.

With a wholesome fear of Governor Cleveland, afterwards, December 1, 1884, those indicted June 30 and July 23, 1884, were called into court, before Judge Moore, when the demurs entered July 8, 1884, were overruled, and the defendants refusing to plead, judgment of conviction was entered against them as follows, to wit :—James E. Kelly, Thomas Murray, John S. Stow, Michael Murray, David Johnson, John Kelly, John T. McDougall, indicted as Dougal McDougall, Mark Jordan, Albert H. Cridge, and James Dunn,—the latter on two indictments.

The following persons also appeared on this date and entered the same demurrer to the indictments as had been entered on the foregoing indictments. Among these were Daniel Wartzfelder, James Varley, F. K. Bradley, T. J. Meehan, Daniel Gleason, William Warring and William McNamara. Frank Rodman failed to appear, while James Fry and the innocent Dougal McDougall pleaded "not guilty."

A STAY GRANTED.

A stay of proceedings was granted by Judge Pratt, December 3, 1884, in the eleven cases where judgment of conviction had been entered, pending an appeal to the General Term of the Supreme Court.

What was done in reference to these cases on appeal ?

The General Term of the Supreme Court at Poughkeepsie, May 11, 1885, by a unanimous decision, sustained the judgment of conviction in all these cases. The following is a copy of the order of affirmance in one case, which will illustrate all :

"At a general term of the New York Supreme Court, held in and for the Second Department, at the Court House in the city of Poughkeepsie on the eleventh day of May, 1885, Present,—Hon. Joseph F. Barnard, P. J.; Hon. Jackson O. Dykeman, Hon. Calvin E. Pratt, J.—The people of the State of New York, respondents, *vs.* James E. Kelly, Thomas Murray, and John S. Stow, appellants.

"The appeal therein having been brought on for argument, after hearing William C. De Witt, Esq., of counsel for the appellants, on their behalf, and James W. Ridgway, District Attorney of Kings County, for the respondents, in their behalf, and due deliberation thereon having been had, it is hereby ordered and adjudged that the judgment of conviction therein rendered by the Court of Sessions of the County of Kings on the 1st day of December, 1884, against the appellants, from which this appeal was taken, be, and the same hereby is, in all respects affirmed."

(Signed by the Clerk.)

The orders of affirmance in these cases were filed in the County Clerk's office of Kings County, June 8, 1885.

GAMBLERS CONTINUED TO PLY THEIR TRADE.

A few days afterwards the agents of the New York Society for the Suppression of Vice found the law being openly violated at Brighton Beach and at the Sheepshead Bay race track the same as before. We secured the evidence, and the Grand Jury, June 25, 1885, indicted the following parties on our complaints, to wit: Michael Murray and two assistants, Thomas Brown and three assistants, Edward Ross and Charles Clifton and their assistants.

Murray, Brown, and Clifton gave bail and returned to business. One other gambler died before arrest. Throughout the summer and fall seasons of 1885 these crimes continued. "Big Mike" Murray was not called for sentence, nor has he, even to this date, been tried upon this new indictment. In not one of the above cases have the witnesses ever been subpœnaed for trial.

June, 1886, the season of the Coney Island Jockey Club again opened. Gamblers resumed business under the "protection combine" of Kings County officials. Again our agents secured the evidence of their crimes, and by pressing the matter before the Grand Jury, June, 1886, had the following gamblers and jockey clubs indicted, to wit:—The Coney Island Jockey Club, the Brighton Beach Racing Association, David J. Johnson, Joseph Cotton, Arthur Hackett, J. E. McDonald, Henry Stedeker, Herman Traub, and several others.

The " flagrant, persistent, and open " violation of law continued ; and yet none of those against whom judgment of
conviction had been entered Dec. 1, 1884, have been sentenced. Not a subsequent indictment has ever been tried.
No action has been taken against the *seventeen* complained of
by our letter of Sept. 18, 1884, to Mr. Ridgway.

We decided to carry the war into Africa. Accordingly the
foregoing letter was sent to Mr. Van Lovan, the foreman of·
the July Grand Jury.

This letter shows how we blackmail gamblers and furnish protection to them. We moved upon the enemy's
works all along the line, and our efforts were valiantly supported by this Grand Inquest.

Going back a little to pick up a single thread of history,
the reader will find after " Big Mike " Murray and his associate gamblers had been indicted, June, 1885, that, July 3,
1885, a

FORMAL NOTICE OF APPEAL

was filed in the County Clerk's office of Kings County in all
the eleven cases where the General Term had affirmed the
judgment of conviction. One case will illustrate all, to wit :

" Court of Sessions, Kings County.—The people, respondents,
against James E. Kelly, Thomas Murray, and John S. Stow, appellants.

" Please take notice that the above-named defendants hereby appeal
to the Court of Appeals from the judgment of the General Term of the
Supreme Court affirming the judgment of conviction rendered by the
Court of Sessions of the County of Kings, on the 1st day of December,
1884, against the appellants, entered herein on the 3rd day of July, 1885,
and from each and every part thereof.

" Dated, July 3, 1885.

        " Yours, etc.,

           " WILLIAM C. DE WITT,

           " JERRY WERNBERG,

                " Attorneys for Appellants.

" To Hon. JAMES W. RIDGWAY, District Attorney,

           " RODNEY THURSBY, Clerk."

In reference to the time of perfecting an appeal from the General Term to the Court of Appeals, note the provisions of the Code of Criminal Procedure, as follows:

"Section 521. MUST BE TAKEN WITHIN ONE YEAR AFTER JUDGMENT. An appeal must be taken within one year after the judgment was rendered."

In reference to the "Transmitting of the papers to the Appellate Court," Section 532 provides as follows:—

"Upon an appeal being taken, the clerk, with whom the notice of appeal is filed, must, within ten days thereafter, without charge, transmit a copy of the notice of appeal and of the judgment roll, as follows: . . . . If it be to the Court of Appeals, to the clerk of that court."
Criminal causes have precedence over all others in all Appellate Courts.

Section 534 then provides concerning the "Dismissal for Irregularity," as follows:—

"Section 534. DISMISSAL FOR WANT OF RETURN. The court may also, upon like motion, dismiss the appeal, if the return be not made, as provided in section five hundred and thirty-two, unless for good cause they enlarge the time for that purpose."

It will be found hereinafter that no stay was granted upon the order of affirmance of the General Term, Supreme Court, of May 11, 1885, until July 26, 1886, and that no returns had been made to the Clerk of the Court of Appeals up to the 19th day of March, 1887, if there has been any down to the present moment.

The July Grand Jury were asked to indict Mr Ridgway for failing "to inform against or prosecute" seventeen gamblers complained of to him as openly violating the law, as named in our first letter to Mr. Ridgway of September 18, 1884. Our witnesses were called, and as a result every one of the seventeen shielded and protected gamblers aforesaid was indicted. It took nearly two years of persistent warfare upon our part to secure any action against gamblers of whom it was charged, in September, 1884, that they had " fixed " everybody so that they would not be interfered with.

Mr. Ridgway was called to a very strict account by the Grand Jury. He was greatly troubled, and it is claimed that, as a compromise, he promised to bring the eleven cases which the General Term had passed upon, as aforesaid (May 11, 1885), into court for sentence.

WHAT WAS DONE?

A notice was served upon these parties July 26, while the Grand Jury was in session, for them to come to court for sentence July 27, 1886. Then more fine work was done. James E. Kelly said, according to the Brooklyn *Union*, June 30, 1884, " The indictments will be pigeon-holed," etc. Did he not know what he was talking about? How easy it is to humbug the public, to find a legal technicality or cover for not enforcing the law! How easy to manipulate and keep convicted criminals from being sentenced!

As will be seen, by reference to the Code and the forego- ing dates, more than " the year " allowed for perfecting these appeals had passed. During this entire period, from May 11, 1885, to July 27, 1886, or taking it from the date the order of affirmance was filed with the County Clerk, June 8, 1885, or even of the notice of appeal, July 3, 1885, more than a year had passed, and all that time NO STAY HAD BEEN GRANTED, so that these convicted criminals could have been sentenced at any time, yet not one has been sentenced.

Instead, what?

Mr. Jere Wernberg, counsel for these men, went to Poughkeepsie on the night train July 26, 1886, and, upon some stipulation by the prosecution, secured a stay of pro- ceedings for the purpose of carrying these cases to the Court of Appeals.

134 GAMBLING OUTRAGES.

July 27, 1886, when the gamblers, who rumor claimed in
June, 1884, were to be protected, and whom James E. Kelly
(the one who it was claimed had made a contract for protection) assured June 30, 1884, that " the indictments would be
pigeon-holed," etc., were called for sentence, the following bit of strategy on their part to further secure these gamblers from sentence was brought forward, to wit:

A STAY BY JUDGE BARNARD.

NEW YORK SUPREME COURT.

THE PEOPLE OF THE STATE OF NEW YORK,
vs.
DOUGAL McDOUGALL.

City of Brooklyn, County of Kings. ss.

I, Hon. Joseph F. Barnard, one of the Justices of the Supreme Court
of the State of New York, do hereby certify that in my opinion there
is reasonable doubt whether the judgment of conviction entered against
the above named defendant in the Court of Sessions of County of Kings
on the first day of December, 1884, on an indictment charging said defendant with registering and recording bets and wagers, and which judgment was affirmed by the General Term of the Supreme Court, should
stand.
Dated *July* 26, 1886.　　　　　　　　　J. F. BARNARD.
[Seal]

(Copy.)　JOHN M. RANKIN,
　　　　　　Clerk.

The certified copy of this certificate of doubt also contained the titles of all the other ten cases against whom
judgment of conviction was entered December 1, 1884.
Afterwards, to wit, Aug. 20, 1886, the following letter was
sent Judge Barnard. We felt that he had been imposed
upon, and determined to undeceive him. We felt bound not
only to inform him of the facts, but to appeal to him for
relief.

August 20, 1886.

Honorable JOSEPH F. BARNARD,
    Justice of the Supreme Court,
        Poughkeepsie, N. Y.

Honorable and Dear Sir :—I beg most respectfully to ask your consideration of the following matter, which I submit strictly to secure the ends of justice, and to lay before your Honor certain facts which I cannot but feel you ought to know.

I am informed that during the present month your Honor has issued a certificate of doubt so as to stay the proceedings in the matter of James E. Kelly and other gamblers, in which cases your Honor rendered a decision on behalf of the General Term of the Supreme Court May 11, 1885. The facts are briefly as follows :

June, 1884, the Grand Jury in and for the Sessions Court of the County of Kings, in Brooklyn, found true bills of indictment against twenty-two (22) gamblers for violating Section 351 of the Penal Code. Nineteen (19) of these gamblers demurred to their indictments, and the demurrer being overruled, judgment of conviction was entered against them. An appeal was taken to the General Term of the Supreme Court in some eleven cases, and the judgment of conviction was affirmed by your honorable Court on the 11th day of May, 1885, in all these cases. The order of affirmance was filed in the County Clerk's office, of the County of Kings, June 8, 1885. A simple notice of appeal was filed in the County Clerk's office on the 3rd of July, 1885, but no appeal was taken other than this, and no judgment roll was filed with the Clerk of the Court of Appeals, nor were any papers sent to the Clerk of the Court of Appeals up to July, 1886, and more than a year passed before any action whatever was taken to perfect this appeal. And I am informed, and verily believe, that the present stay of proceedings is not asked of your Honor for the purposes of securing the ends of justice, but rather to further protect and screen gamblers who have all these years been permitted to go unwhipped of justice, while they have continued to openly transgress and violate the laws of the State of New York, in the County of Kings, by committing the same crimes for which they were indicted in June, 1884. The facts disclose a most disgraceful and shameful condition of affairs in that county.

I now most respectfully ask permission to lay before your Honor the following history of these disgraceful proceedings :

During the months of June and September of each year the Coney Island Jockey Club, at the town of Gravesend, in the County of Kings, permit their premises to be occupied and used by gamblers, nearly all of whom are non-residents of Kings County, and some non-residents of the State of New York, who come there and openly violate Section 351 of the Penal Code by selling pools and registering bets and wagers on horse races. In June, 1884, I secured evidence against twenty-two (22) of these gamblers. I drew the complaints according to due form of law. These complaints were taken to the District Attorney on the 23d of June, 1884. The District Attorney, Mr. Ridgway, promised absolutely to take up these matters on the 25th and personally bring them before the Grand Jury, advising against any warrants to arrest or seize their unlawful paraphernalia, and promising that the next morning after the Grand Jury should take action he would have bench warrants and search warrants ready to arrest the parties who should be indicted and to seize their unlawful paraphernalia, which they then and there kept and publicly used in violation of law.

On the 25th the witnesses, having been notified, were in attendance, but instead of being called, were allowed to wait the entire day without being called. Mr. Ridgway did not appear at all, nor could he be found. On the 26th day of June, upon my earnest demand that the matter be considered, one case was taken up out of the twenty-two (22) which we had prepared, and the witnesses were then instructed that they need not wait, as nothing more would be done that day. The witnesses did go away, but afterwards returned to the First Assistant District Attorney in charge of the Grand Jury, the same day, and demanded of him to promptly take these matters before the Grand Jury or we would go at once to the Governor of the State; whereupon the witnesses were called at once, and all the twenty-two (22) gamblers were· indicted. Matters, however, were delayed, so that it was the 30th day of June, or the last day but one of the races for the June season of 1884, before the indictments were filed.

When the indictments were filed it was found that eleven (11) of these gamblers had been notified, and were in waiting in the District Attorney's office with their bondsmen ready to give bail. Bench warrants were issued against the others, and I went to Mr. Ridgway for search warrants, as these men continued to boldly violate the law, not even being checked by the action of the Grand Jury. To my amazement and surprise, Mr. Ridgway, the District Attorney, informed me that no search warrants would be issued, and that the men who had been indicted would not be arrested; but that one of Mr. Ridgway's officers would go down to the race track where these men were and would notify them to appear, if I would send one of the witnesses to identify the men indicted to the officer who held the bench warrants. I protested to Mr. Ridgway against this course of procedure, because it was irregular ; and I told him further,

LETTER TO JUSTICE BARNARD.

as a reason why it ought not to be done, that it was rumored and openly charged that the gamblers had paid $50,000 not to be arrested, and that an agreement had been made—because of the payment of this money—that they should not be arrested nor interfered with during the racing season, and I urged these rumors and charges as a reason why these men ought to be arrested and their unlawful matter seized. Instead, however, these men were not arrested, but an officer went down with a witness who could identify the indicted gamblers, and while the gamblers were openly violating the law and stood there with their paraphernalia for registering and recording bets and wagers in full and open view, the officer and the witness went from booth to booth, and as the witness pointed out the gambler, the gambler ceased his gambling operations long enough to be notified by said officer that he had been indicted, the name under which he had been indicted, and for him to appear the next morning and give bail. Their gambling paraphernalia was not seized; their unlawful business was not interfered with other than as above; and the men who had given bail in the morning, as mentioned above, were there with these other men, committing the same offence, the same afternoon, and have continued to violate the law since.

In September, 1884, these same men having continued to violate the law, I sent three men down to the race track, and these three men secured positive and aosolute evidence against seventeen (17) gamblers, thirteen (13) of whom had been indicted in June previous. Complaints were drawn according to due form of law, the exhibits were attached, and Mr. Ridgway was notified by a letter, copy of which is enclosed and marked "Exhibit A," but no action was taken.

In June, the next season, these same gamblers opened business, and we secured evidence against them, and by dint of great pressure had these parties indicted for the offences of June, 1885, but could not get the cases of September, 1884, acted upon. I may add here as a fact that the District Attorney has not, down to the present time, ever subpœnaed one of these witnesses before any Court or Grand Jury in those cases of September, 1884; and it was not until July, 1886, just previous to their application for a stay to your Honor, when I preferred charges against James W. Ridgway, the District Attorney, to the Grand Jury, and demanded that these cases be taken up and acted upon, that these seventeen (17) cases, together with three others, were taken up by the Grand Jury and indictments were found against them. This, let it be remembered, was nearly two years after the crimes had been committed, and after Mr. Ridgway had been informed of these facts and furnished with the names of the defendants and the names of the witnesses.

During the months of June and September of the years 1884, 1885, and the month of June, 1886, gambling has been permitted to be carried on without let or hindrance by notorious professional gamblers in Kings County, not only upon the Coney Island Jockey Club race track at Sheepshead Bay, but also, as it is now being carried on, on the race course of the Brighton Beach Racing Association at Brighton Beach, both in the town of Gravesend, in the County of Kings.

For years the newspapers have demanded the enforcement of these laws, and have published the facts concerning the scandalous and outrageous proceedings in the courts and out of the courts in reference to these cases in that county.

I present to your Honor the fact that while these men have been under judgment of conviction, and with no stay to prevent their being sentenced, they have not been called for sentence until I demanded the indictment of James W. Ridgway for non-performance of his duty, and for violating Section 349 of the Penal Code, in that he, having reason to believe that that Section was being violated, has not informed against or prosecuted the men who he knew were violating the law.

It will thus be observed that professional gamblers indicted in June, 1884, have continued to violate the law ever since; that though subsequently complained of to the District Attorney, he would not permit any proceedings to be taken, nor has he subpœnaed a single witness before any Court or Grand Jury against these gamblers whom he had reason to believe were continuing to violate the law in September, after the Grand Jury had indicted them in June, 1884.

Again, it must be observed that indictments found against these same gamblers in June, 1885, have not one of them been tried in the Sessions Court.

Again, after the General Term of the Supreme Court had affirmed the conviction, and more than a year has elapsed since that order was filed in the County Clerk's office of the County of Kings, these men have remained unsentenced; nor am I aware of a single instance where any motion has been made to have them sentenced except as aforesaid, nor had there been any papers filed with the Clerk of the Court of Appeals in these cases up to July, 1886. In July, 1886, I demanded the indictment of James W. Ridgway, the District Attorney, for violation of Section 349, of the Penal Code, and for protecting and shielding the gamblers and preventing the enforcement of the law while they openly and scandalously violated it. After the year to which by law they are entitled to perfect their appeal has passed, now they appeal to your Honor, I know not upon what grounds, for a certificate of doubt in order that these men may go unwhipped of justice, their business be not interfered with, while they transgress the laws of this State and bring scandal and reproach upon the administration of justice in the County of Kings.

Thinking that your Honor would not intentionally lend yourself to any disgraceful proceedings such as have characterized the administration of justice in reference to these gamblers in Kings County, I feel it my duty to lay before your Honor these facts, and ask, if it be consistent with the enforcement of law, that the certificate of doubt which your Honor has issued in these cases may be revoked.

Your Honor will perceive that there will be no likelihood of any application being made on the part of the District Attorney or the Court of Sessions, who have thus notoriously allowed these crimes to go on, who have, in the face of monstrous scandals, permitted these laws to be violated; and I call attention to this one fact, that Judge Moore, in charging the Grand Jury, June 2, 1884, said to them, as was reported in all the papers at the time, that "the violation of law in the town of Gravesend against gambling was flagrant, persistent, and open."

I enclose you also copy of a letter which I sent to Judge Moore, July 11, 1884, which showed him clearly how these laws have been transgressed and exposes some of the scandalous proceedings that had been had up to that time, but nothing has been done thus far to stop these outrages by way of punishing offending parties.

I beg further to present one thing for your consideration, that after the Governor's proclamation, in the fall of 1881, calling upon the courts to enforce the law against gambling, I secured over fifty-five (55) indictments, in the Sessions Court of Kings County, against common gamblers, who were indicted for violating Section 344 of the Penal Code, which makes the offence a felony. The evidence in most of these cases is of the most absolute and positive character, being supported by two or more witnesses. In the face, however, of the Governor's proclamation and this positive evidence, over fifty (50) indictments against these felons were dismissed, and without just cause these felons were allowed to escape the penalty of the law for their crimes, by the Sessions Court, in December, 1883. Some of these indictments had only been found in September, 1883, or about three months previous to their being dismissed.

To illustrate: one man named Philipps, a special policeman, was found writing "lottery-policy," in violation of Section 344. There was one witness who purchased the policy, and two other witnesses who immediately entered the premises where this man was violating the law and seized the manifold-book with the play recorded which he had just sold, and caught him in the act of writing other policies which he was then selling to persons there in the place as the officers entered. Another man arrested the same afternoon named Foster,—the same facts are true concerning his case, except that he was not a special policeman; and yet these are two of the indictments that were dismissed by this Court without any regard to the proof.

Again, out of more than one hundred (100) indictments which I have secured the evidence for, that have been found in the Sessions Court for Kings County, but one of all that number was ever brought to trial, convicted, and sentenced in the Sessions Court of Kings County.

In view of these facts, it must be manifest to your Honor that if a wrong has been done in the application for a stay of proceedings, or certificate of doubt in reference to gambling cases, whatever imposition may have been made upon your Honor, will not be rectified by any representative of the people in the District Attorney's office of Kings County.

I have deemed it my duty to lay these facts, the evidence of which is within my own knowledge, before your Honor, and to ask that they may be considered by you, and such action taken as these facts and the law in the premises will warrant and permit.

Will not the Judges of the Supreme Court of the District of Kings County order an Oyer and Terminer Court to examine into all of these outrages against law and justice and try these indictments now pending, to the end that these laws may be enforced, that public gambling shall cease, and that men who have so long defied the laws may be taught that the laws cannot be violated with impunity?

If your Honor desires, I shall esteem it a pleasure to call upon you at any time that you may name and produce witnesses to substantiate and prove the facts as set out in this letter.

Trusting that you will pardon the length of this communication and the liberty I have taken in addressing you, I remain, with an earnest desire to secure the proper enforcement of the law, and with very great respect,

Your most obedient servant,

(Signed)   ANTHONY COMSTOCK,

Secretary.

In reply to this letter Justice Barnard very courteously responded.

LETTER FROM JUSTICE BARNARD.

A. COMSTOCK:

Dear Sir:—I have read your letter. The case before me was this: There were a number of convictions for a common offence. One was appealed and argued and decided. The others were also appealed, but by agreement between the accused and the law officers of Kings County were not formally argued, but were to abide the result of the one case argued, as all were precisely alike. The case argued was appealed to the Court of Appeals, and the stipulation coming, I certified probable cause for the appeal. This certificate necessarily stayed the case which was argued, and also all the cases which depended upon it. I think the conviction is right and will be sustained, but the Appellate Court may differ from this.

Yours,

J. F. BARNARD.

This reply lets a little light upon this rather extraordinary proceeding. It is natural to ask : Did Mr. Ridgway act in good faith with the Grand Jury? Was there an agreement or contract for protection to these gamblers, or was there a faithful discharge of his duty under his oath of office? Was not the appeal irregular? Could there be a legal appeal? More than a year had elapsed since the General Term affirmed the judgment of conviction. Was there a stipulation between Mr. Ridgway and the counsel for the defendants? If so, what?

Another letter was sent Justice Barnard, as follows :

TANNERSVILLE, *Aug.* 29, 1886.

Hon. JOSEPH F. BARNARD,
    Justice Supreme Court,
        Poughkeepsie, N. Y.

Dear Sir :—I haste to make grateful acknowledgment of your esteemed favor of the 27th inst. May I ask if there was a stipulation made before your Honor, or any papers filed July 26, 1886, for a stay of the proceedings in the case of People *vs.* James E. Kelly *et al.?* If so, I ask that you will allow your clerk to forward a copy of all the papers to me, certified. I will remit all fees as soon as he shall forward the same to me.

There are two points in these cases which have very great force to my mind.

First. For more than a year, while these gamblers have continued to violate the law, they have been permitted to go unsentenced, without any *stay* to prevent their being sentenced ; and no appeal has been perfected or paper filed with the Clerk of the Court of Appeals.

Second. They were not moved for sentence until after the Grand Jury, in July last, had called Mr. Ridgway to account, and until a demand for the indictment of Mr. Ridgway had been made. As soon as he moved then (when he was forced to move), they apply for a stay, when they had allowed *more than a year* to elapse without perfecting their appeal or filing any papers with the Court of Appeals. This order of affirmance was made May 11, 1885.

The stay was asked for July 26, 1886.

Should not the appeal have been completed within a year after the affirmance of the General Term, according to the Code of Criminal Procedure?

During the present month another set of men have opened another race course, in the little town of Gravesend, making now three places where professional gamblers openly and flagrantly violate and defy the laws. The constituted authorities will not enforce these laws until forced to do so. No action was taken upon the affirmance of judgment of the General Term any more than if you had not decided the case. When forced to move, they shelter themselves behind a stay. I cannot but feel that there is no good faith in this, but rather a conspiracy on the part of the District Attorney and the counsel for these gamblers and the gamblers themselves that they shall not be sentenced nor their unlawful business interfered with.

From my knowledge of these cases and my conversation with Mr. Ridgway, and the rumors of "fixing things" by the payment of large sums of money by these gamblers, I cannot but believe and feel that the whole matter, so far as concerns the local authorities, lacks good faith and only confirms the scandalous charges, so often made, that there had been agreements made by which Mr. Ridgway would protect and shield these men from consequences of violated law.

I respectfully submit that for a hundred or more indictments to remain untried while the prisoners continue to violate the law is to bring a sad reproach upon the administration of justice.

Cannot something be done by the Judges of the Supreme Court to correct this evil? I have the honor to be

Your most obedient servant,

(Signed) ANTHONY COMSTOCK,

Secretary.

The Judges of the Supreme Court may order a term of the Oyer and Terminer Court to be held at any time, and the law requires a Grand Jury to be called each term. This

last is true, as I am informed by lawyers, in some counties of the State at least, if not in all.

To this letter the Justice makes reply as follows:

A. COMSTOCK:

Dear Sir :—I do not remember the particular titles, but there were
papers showing an appeal in due form, and a stipulation that the case on
appeal was to determine the other cases. If the appeal was taken in
the main case within the year, it would operate under the stipulation to
stay the others until that was decided, if there was a certificate of probable cause for the appeal. The papers should be on file in the Kings
County Clerk's office. No doubt the appeal can be heard Oct. 6, 1886,
when the Court of Appeals meets.

Yours truly,

J. F. BARNARD.

We have not been able to find the moving papers above
referred to.

As to the appeal, and whether the stay should not even
now be reconsidered, read the following letter to the Clerk of
the Court of Appeals, sent the last week in January, 1887 :

NEW YORK, *Jan.* 27, 1887.

CLERK OF THE COURT OF APPEALS,

Albany, N. Y.

Dear Sir:—I would respectfully ask that you will inform me, on the
receipt of this, if there has been any judgment roll, or appeal papers, filed
in the following cases, to wit :

People *vs.* James E. Kelly,

"   "   Michael Murray,

"   "   John S. Stow,

"   "   Thomas Murray,

"   "   John Kelly,

"   "   John T. McDougall, alias Dougal McDougall,

"   "   David Johnson,

"   "   Alfred H. Cridge,

"   "   Martin Jordan,

"   "   James Dunn.

Very respectfully yours,

(Signed) ANTHONY COMSTOCK,

Secretary,

Per S.

To this letter Mr. Perrin, the Clerk of the Court of Appeals, replied upon its back as follows, and his reply was received January 29, 1887, to wit :

NO RETURNS OR APPEAL PAPERS FILED YET.

ALBANY, *Jan.* 28, 1887.
ANTHONY COMSTOCK, Esq.,
         Secretary, etc.
Dear Sir :—Returns on appeal to the Court of Appeals in *none* of the above cases have been filed in this office.
         Respectfully,
            E. O. PERRIN,
            Clerk of the Court of Appeals,
               State of New York.

Later, upon the witness stand, under another oath taken by him before the Bacon Investigating Committee, March 19, 1887, Mr. Ridgway swears that the Kelly and other cases are " pending in the Court of Appeals," whereupon Mr. W. W. Goodrich produced a certificate from Mr. E. O. Perrin, Clerk of the Court of Appeals, showing that in none of the eleven cases decided by the General Term, May 11, 1885, have any returns whatever been received by him or in his office.

One more item calls for attention in this connection.

In response to Specification 13 of Charge 1 against Mr. Ridgway charging that " he did administer the laws in the interest of gamblers by refusing to cause their arrest and prosecute them before a committing magistrate while they were openly violating Section 351 of the Penal Code, and by refusing to allow bench warrants to be executed against said gamblers, and by refusing to allow their unlawful business to be interfered with on the *30th day of June,* 1884, but did allow said gamblers to continue to violate the law, the said Ridgway notifying them through his officers to appear and give bail on the first day of July, " etc., Mr. Ridgway makes answer, under oath, as follows :—

" Respondent denies the same, and avers that in every instance where indictments had been found by the Grand Jury, and before they could be filed and bench warrants issued, the officers employed by Anthony Comstock, who are his constant associates, repaired to the race track and there informed the persons they had complained against that indictments had been found and that bench warrants would be issued for their arrest."

To this we reply : This statement is maliciously false and known to Mr. Ridgway *to be false.*

He further says :—" A large number of indictments were found against John Doe and Richard Roe, whose names the said witnesses asserted that they did not know, and that they demanded that the District Attorney should issue the bench warrants to them for execution. That respondent believed that they desired to make use of the processes of the court for improper purposes, and believing many public rumors that they, in conjunction with Anthony Comstock, were engaged in blackmailing such offenders, respondent refused to give them the bench warrants for execution, and placed them in the hands of the Sheriff of the County of Kings. And that respondent is informed and verily believes that it is because respondent refused to permit the processes of the court to be used by the said Comstock and his assistants for blackmailing purposes that these charges have been made and are now made against respondent. "

There are two or three things in this connection which I ask the reader to consider :

First—There were no indictments found at that time nor that year against " John Doe " or " Richard Roe. " Mr. Ridgway could not produce a single indictment found in June, 1884 (to which these charges refer), or in any part of 1884, containing the name of a single gambler indicted as " John Doe " or " Richard Roe" before the Bacon Investigating Committee. And not one appears upon the list he himself produced and put in evidence.

Secondly—Mr. Ridgway was never asked to give us the bench warrants.

Thirdly—That is not our way of dealing with blackmailers or blackmailing schemes.

At that time there had been boasts made by the gamblers, at least rumors of boasts made by the gamblers, that they had not only my office, but Mr. Ridgway's office, "fixed" so that they would not be interfered with. The writer took these rumors to Mr. Ridgway, June 23, 1884, Mr. W. C. Beecher being present. As has been shown, we sent down to the race course and secured the evidence against twenty-two of the principal gamblers, took the evidence and the witnesses to Mr. Ridgway, and demanded of him that these men forthwith be arrested and their gambling paraphernalia seized. We also urged as a reason why prompt action should be taken the fact that these scandalous rumors were in circulation. It will be seen that we did succeed in overcoming the antipathy to interfere with the gambling business, by threats of going directly to Governor Cleveland, sufficiently to have twenty-two of the gamblers indicted; and then a peace officer conveyed to them the compliments of the District Attorney and invited them to come up to his office and give bail, which was done against our protest.

But this was not all. As soon as the September or fall season of 1884 opened at Sheepshead Bay fresh rumors were set afloat that the

GAMBLERS HAD EVERYBODY " FIXED."

What we did then by advertising a reward, by securing the evidence against the very men whom it was charged had paid us $2500 as the price of our silence, our fight for more than two years to get these men into court, are all before the reader. Would we have contended for the prosecution of these gamblers, in face of bitterest opposition, had they paid us money for our silence? Do blackmailers press criminals to the bar of justice after they have extorted money from them, especially, as in this case, where the gamblers and District Attorney were both *hostile* and all looking for points and means to down them, and particularly where the receiving of such money is a State's-prison offence? Not so.

Blackmailers do not prosecute criminals in courts after they have committed a crime by receiving the criminals' money.

If money is the motive that actuates the agents of the Society for the Suppression of Vice, it would not be necessary for us to put ourselves in the hands of gamblers who are protected by officials. Such a process is rather hazardous. Blackmailers do not generally demand protection money from criminals who have the ear, friendship, and protection of District Attorneys and other executive officers.

If we had desired money considerations, we need not to have waited until this late day.

In the case of the gilded palace on Fifth Avenue, kept by the notorious Madame Restell, that was suppressed through the efforts of the agents of this Society, a gentleman who was at that time her attorney, and who to-day occupies an official position in the City of New York, says he had placed in his hands $40,000 in cash, to be paid to the writer to secure his co-operation in a scheme to protect the wretched proprietress of that establishment from criminal prosecution.

Upon another occasion a gentleman called at our office, who was very solicitous for our health, and wanted to know if I would not like to take a trip around the world with my family. When told, " I could not afford it," he was exceedingly interested to know from me, " if my salary for five years was paid in advance and a handsome sum for travelling expenses was deposited with it to my order in my bank, if I would not make the excursion?"

There is a standing offer from one lottery company, whom we had driven out of the City of New York and forced to close their doors, of $25,000 cash a year if we will not interfere with them if they open a lottery office in this city.

One notorious fraud, who had an income of more than $1000 a day through the mail, and whose fraudulent operatinos were suppressed through this office, sent his emissaries to our office with an offer of $20,000 if we would allow his schemes to continue through the mail and not interfere with him.

Money is the potent power by which crime is allowed to exist. It is a subtle secret influence often applied by gamblers and other criminals to secure immunity from arrest and prosecution.

We have neither protected crimes nor blackmailed criminals.

If we had, does any one suppose that our enemies would not have secured the fact and used it against us? The gambler knows when he is blackmailed and to whom he pays the levy. With hundreds of criminals convicted by us during the past fifteen years, does any one suppose for one moment that if there had been any crime committed by us, it would not have been proven years ago, and not be left for an official, writhing under the lash of public scorn for failure to do his duty, to insinuate it by his " I heard so"

Does Mr. Ridgway intend the public to understand that after all the favors he has shown the gamblers since January 1, 1884, when he first went into office, he and they together have only " I heard so " to support his base insinuations? I leave the public to say.

In summing up, we find that professional gamblers from outside the County of Kings for years have been permitted to go into Kings County and openly violate the law.   James

E. Kelly, the "boss" gambler, with comforting words—
and his statements have not been denied in any public manner, that I have been able to discover—told his men June
30, 1884, that "these indictments will be pigeon-holed
and we have nothing to fear; in any case our business will
not be interfered with this season." Complaints are borne
to the District Attorney's office that "it is charged that these
men have made a bargain, that they have paid $50,000, and
in consideration of the said money they were not to be interfered with." Yet, in the face of these rumors, confirmed
by the statements of James E. Kelly and the extraordinary
proceedings in these cases, not a single one of all these cases
has been prosecuted to judgment of sentence. Indictment
after indictment has been permitted to be filed and remain
pigeon-holed; eleven cases where no stay of proceedings
was granted from May 11, 1885, to July 26, 1886, remain
unsentenced; these same indicted gamblers were permitted
to go right on violating the law, with subsequent indictments
for subsequent offences found in the mean time, in the same
court, untried,—and yet *not one of these men has been to this
writing tried on subsequent indictments nor sentenced on the
judgment of conviction.*

Can such things as these be permitted in an enlightened
community and be tolerated or sanctioned when the facts
are known? Must the writer lose his reputation for truth
and veracity before the people because he has untiringly
and persistently endeavored by due process of law to stop
gambling?

Are we to be execrated because we have dared to stem
this tide of corruption and expose this official's neglect and
rottenness? If that be the verdict, after reading this record
of facts, then let the hand of vengeance fall; we still have
he comfort and consolation of having done at least something to crush out these evils. We appeal to the public for
their verdict.

CHAPTER IX.

WHITEWASHED.

AFTER Mr. Ridgway's arduous duties in acquitting Dougal McDougall, the innocent, in place of John T., the guilty, after John T. had had a judgment of conviction entered against him in the same court for the offence set out in the indictment upon which Dougal, the innocent, was tried, Mr. Ridgway bethought him of another strategic movement by which he was to secure for himself a "karacter." The Grand Jury applied a coat of

WHITEWASH.

The January Grand Jury of 1885 made a presentment to the Court as follows:

After citing several "Whereas" as to where they derived their information and what they had done, the Grand Jury say:

"The Grand Jury does further present that there does not now exist in any precinct of said county, so far as the authorities know, any gambling house, room or premises; that so far as an honest and energetic discharge of official duty can accomplish such a result, the City of Brooklyn and County of Kings is entirely free from all gambling houses, rooms, or premises of every description; that the present administration of the law by all of said authorities is most efficient and energetic; and that the District Attorney's office of the county has been and now is administered honestly, vigorously, and thoroughly, and in full loyalty to the public welfare.

(Signed) " HERBERT W. CLAPP,
" (Foreman), with Eighteen Grand Jurors."

This was in itself so ridiculous that the papers denounced it as a "whitewashing" scheme.

First, note the fact that not a witness was called from the New York Society for the Suppression of Vice to testify as to facts within their knowledge.

Secondly, charges were then pending before the Governor against Mr. Ridgway and his administration.

Thirdly, the following advertisement appeared in one or more papers during the time that this Grand Jury were in session, to wit :

POOL—SELLING OPENLY ADVERTISED.

" SPORTING : New Orleans races commence Tuesday, January 26. *Auction, Mutual, Combination Pools, book-making at Paul Bauer's* Club House, West Brighton, Coney Island. Telegraph orders receive prompt attention. Take Sea Beach route. Races, Wednesday and Friday of each week. Sea Beach railroad tickets good on race days."

In this connection it will be of interest to read the letter to Mr. Ridgway of September 18, on page 103, which contained the names and residences of witnesses against seventeen gamblers whom he would not permit to be brought before any Grand Jury. Consider Dougal the innocent. Then say whether the foreman of the Grand Jury and eighteen members, under their oaths, could certify that " the present administration of the law by all of said authorities is most efficient and energetic, and that the District Attorney's office of the county has been and now is administered honestly, vigorously, and thoroughly, and in full loyalty to the public welfare."

Let it be remembered that none of the witnesses against the gamblers named in the letter of the eighteenth of September, 1884, were examined by this Grand Jury. Not one had been examined at all concerning the offences committed in September, 1884, by the gamblers who had been indicted in June.

The chief editor of the Brooklyn *Union* had been called as a witness, and in their presentment the Grand Jury say,

"Has summoned before it the chief editor of said newspaper, who after having been examined upon them, testified that he had no knowledge of the existence of any gambling place within the boundary of Kings County."

This presentment was filed on the thirtieth day of January, 1885. The Brooklyn *Union* of January 31, 1885, in speaking of the presentment of the Grand Jury, says :

"The editor of the *Union* begs to repeat that he has no personal knowledge of the existence of such at the present time, though he is credibly assured by those whose tastes or opportunities for observation differ from his that card gambling was never carried to such lengths as just now in Brooklyn. But the editor *offered to furnish the District Attorney*, and hereby offers to furnish any Grand Jury desiring to get at the facts, with the testimony of those members of the staff of the *Union* who have been detailed to visit and describe the pool-rooms at Coney Island. He would direct attention to the evidence supplied by Mr. Comstock from the advertising columns of a New York newspaper that pools are now being sold at Paul Bauer's," etc.

As the result of a letter to the Brooklyn *Eagle*, above referred to, I am very happy to record something of interest in favor of Mr. Ridgway. On February 4 a man named George Miller was arrested at Paul Bauer's place. No pools were being sold, but Miller was cashing in pool tickets for those that held winners. He was arrested. Afterwards Mr. Paul Bauer came forward to go his bail. Bauer unwittingly admitted that he was the proprietor of the place where the pool-gambling was advertised as being carried on, and thereupon Mr. Bauer was indicted on the tenth day of February and arrested. He was subsequently convicted and sentenced by Judge Moore to three months' imprisonment and $750 fine. After sentence Mr. Bauer paid his fine and then appealed from the judgment, on the ground that he had been illegally sentenced; that "the judge erred in sentencing him to less than one year's imprisonment," under Section 351 of the Penal Code. He was brought out on habeas corpus proceedings and appealed to the General Term of the Supreme Court, which at Poughkeepsie, May 25, 1885, by a unanimous decision, sustained the judgment.— (People *vs.* Bauer, 37 Hun.) Mr. Bauer, however, has been shielded from the further serving of his sentence, and still walks the streets of Kings County a free man, notwithstand-the decision of the General Term.

POLICY GAMBLERS ALSO SHIELDED.

The same day that Mr. Bauer was arrested we secured the arrest of John E. Cummings, a common gambler, who kept a policy and gambling place at 170 Skillman Street, where we seized a large amount of paraphernalia, including the manifold-books upon which the policy which he had just sold was recorded. When the officer and the writer entered the premises we found him sitting at a table writing policies —engaged in the act. One of my assistants had just purchased a policy, and the record of the same was found on the table in front of Cummings; and yet notwithstanding all this evidence John E. Cummings has never been brought to trial.

Prior to this, two persons had been arrested in Clinton Street for keeping a gambling saloon there, one named Theophilus Gilman and the other Buckley. These men when arrested were found in possession of the place with the gambling paraphernalia in their possession. The witnesses had previously been in and seen the gambling games going on. Besides all this, when these men were arraigned before the committing magistrate, Mr. Gilman pleaded "guilty;" yet neither of these men has been prosecuted thus far. These cases were pending at the time of the filing of this present-ment by the Grand Jury.

These cases illustrate the "honest and vigorous"

manner in which the District Attorney had discharged his duty, as set forth by the foreman of the Grand Jury and eighteen members aforesaid.

The indictments against pool gamblers of Brighton Beach, John Y. McKane, chief of police, and eight of his subordinates, indicted Sept., 1883, remained untried, while gambling had continued at that race course for 125 days during the year 1884, if the official turf guide is to be believed. Had this Grand Jury knowledge of these facts? We do not believe it. They were simply manipulated, by some one in Mr. Ridgway's interests. *It was all for effect upon the public mind.*

As long as the public can be hoodwinked rascalities pay better than the faithful discharge of duty. Let the mask be torn away. Open the dark dungeon door which is sought to be hermetically sealed so that the public cannot see, and let the light in upon these whited sepulchres. It is time to call a halt all along the line.

CHARGES TO THE GOVERNOR.

As has been seen, Nov., 1884, when we found that nothing could be done to enforce the law in Kings County, not even upon those whom we had secured indictments against, the Executive Committee of the New York Society for the Suppression of Vice appealed to Governor Cleveland.

It must be remembered that we could not get our first twenty-two cases before the Grand Jury, even after Mr. Ridgway's letter and public proclamation of April and May, 1884, and Judge Moore's charge to the Grand Jury of June 3, 1884, until we threatened to go direct to the Governor of the State.

As the result of the appeal of the Executive Committee, the gamblers were brought into Court Dec. 1, 1884, and their demurs overruled.

But it is said we did not press our charges. What was done, and why?

Governor Cleveland had been called to the highest gift of the nation. He had been elected President of the United States. This necessarily involved a suspension of many duties connected with the executive office of the State. In his preparations for a higher and more important duty he had not time, nor could it have been reasonably expected of him, to take up our charges, but rather he referred them to his successor in office. Supplemental charges were filed concerning the substituting of innocent Dougal McDougall, of New York, in place of guilty John T. McDougall, of Hoboken.

A committee of Messrs. H. E. Simmons, W. C. Beecher, and myself were appointed to press these charges before Governor Hill. Mr. Simmons and myself went to Albany and had an interview with him some time in January or February, 1885, after he had had a little time to straighten out matters appertaining to his office.

Governor Hill suggested that we should take all the papers and unite the two charges together and return the same to him. We took the papers intending to do so. A day or two after we reached New York one of our committee received a letter from Mr. Ridgway containing a promise and pledge to do all in his power to break up gambling.

We had no personal animosity against Mr. Ridgway. We sought the enforcement of the law; we were willing to meet him more than half way and co-operate most heartily. We therefore withdrew our charges entirely and accepted Mr. Ridgway's promise. Read his letter as follows :—

OFFICE OF THE DISTRICT ATTORNEY, COURT HOUSE, ROOM 3.
KINGS COUNTY, BROOKLYN, N. Y.
February 10, 1885.

WILLIAM C. BEECHER, Esq.,
My Dear Sir :—
Some days since my attention was called to an article in the Brooklyn *Times* in which you are reported as having said that you would gladly

render any service that might contribute to destroy the business of pool-
selling at Coney Island. I take this opportunity of saying to you that
it is my intention to give personally my time to the destruction of this
business, and from this time forth I will exert all the power contained in
this office to effect such a result. And I will be pleased if you will call .
my attention to any future violation of the gambling laws in this county
. and give me the benefit of such evidence as you may secure. I have
notified the officers of the several race tracks that they must not permit
pools to be sold upon their tracks, and if at the opening of the season
they disregard the notification, I will proceed against them in such. a
way that I think will drive it from the county forever.

Very respectfully yours,
James W. Ridgway.

The season would not open at the best until June, 1885.
We waited till that time. In the mean time the appeals
of these eleven gamblers who had appealed Dec., 1884,
together with the case of Paul Bauer, who also appealed,
had been argued in the Supreme Court, and June 8, 1885,
the order of affirmance was filed in the County Clerk's office
in Brooklyn.

We secured new indictments against some of the gamblers for offences committed June, 1885, and they were
duly apprehended. Everything promised well. So long as
it did we were willing to wait, test Mr. Ridgway's good faith,
and give him our support. He kept promising to call these
indicted parties to trial. We waited. It went on until June,
1886, and none of the cases appealed had reached the Court
of Appeals, not a gambler had been tried, and their unlawful business kept right on.

It was then determined to carry the matter again to the
Governor, with new and additional charges. It required
much time to prepare these papers, and besides we thought
the shortest way was to have Mr. Ridgway indicted. Then
came the cases in June and July, 1886, and after that a
most responsible duty, which called us away from New
York to Saratoga for two weeks and more. It was not

until September 10, 1886, that we could complete these papers and file them with the Governor.

CHARGES BEFORE GOVERNOR HILL AGAINST MR. RIDGWAY.

Charges and specifications were filed with Governor Hill Sept. 10, 1886, and the removal of Mr. Ridgway demanded thereon. At an interview had with the Governor at the Hoffman House, New York City, in October following, the Governor informed the writer that ' he had read the charges and specifications, and that if they were proven there was enough to remove two district attorneys ; that he had not served a copy of the papers upon Mr. Ridgway, and desired a conference upon the subject of not taking action until after the election. As a reason why he would not take action, the Governor said he did not desire to take any action that might prejudice the coming election ; that Mr. Ridgway, if re-elected, could be as well removed after the first of January as before the expiration of his then present term, that it would necessarily occupy considerable time before the case could be brought to a conclusion, and therefore he did not think it best to take any action until after election ; that if Mr. Ridgway should be re-elected, and after election wè still desired to take action against him, that he would move at once upon our demand.' The idea advanced was, that this was a political movement upon our part. This was emphatically denied. After this interview the matter was laid before the Executive Committee of the New York Society for the Suppression of Vice, and the following letter was sent to Governor Hill, defining our position. The committee directed that an additional copy of the charges and specifications should be forwarded in order that the Governor might have an extra copy to serve upon Mr. Ridgway and thus prevent delay.

LETTER TO GOVERNOR HILL.

NEW YORK, *Oct.* 13, 1886.

To His Excellency
    DAVID B. HILL,
        Governor of the State of New York,
        Albany, N. Y.

Dear Sir :—At a meeting of the executive committee of this Society held yesterday afternoon at these rooms, I was advised by those present to send you a copy of the charges and specifications filed in your office on the 10th day of September last, and to respectfully say to you that in no way can our action be justly construed as a political movement.

In presenting these charges, it has been done because of the corrupt conduct, as we firmly believe, of Mr. Ridgway, in failing to discharge the duties of his office ; and owing to his neglect to enforce these laws new gambling schemes and devices have been adopted and have been allowed to continue, and the laws have been allowed to be violated both before and since the filing of these charges, without being interfered with.

I am directed by the gentlemen also to ask that your Excellency will forthwith serve upon Mr. Ridgway these charges and specifications. And as a special reason why it should be done we enclose you herewith an article published in the Brooklyn *Citizen*, of Kings County, under date of October 6, showing that Mr. Ridgway is making political capital out of the fact that your Excellency has not served these charges upon him.

I understood you to say in that interview that if the charges were proven there was sufficient to remove two district attorneys.

I respectfully submit that this is a serious matter ; that in the entire term of Mr. Ridgway, now nearly three years, he has wilfully neglected to enforce these laws which the Legislature of the State, by Section 349, made it his imperative duty to enforce. Mr. Ridgway in this article says : " There is absolutely nothing in these charges which I cannot answer and dispose of in twenty-four hours after they are served. They come from such an unimportant and unreliable source, and their purport is so obvious, that Governor Hill has never even served them. The public has been led to believe that these charges have been served. Such is not the case. I am ready to meet them at any time."

I respectfully submit, that with charges as serious as these, pending since the 10th of September, with the open violations of law continuing in

Kings County, with unsentenced gamblers continuing to defy the same laws for which they stand convicted; and with indictment after indictment against the same men and these same indictments remaining untried while the gamblers continue to violate the law : these in themselves are sufficient reasons why these charges should be considered, irrespective of any election or nomination which may possibly come to the man who has failed to enforce the laws, and also that these charges should be served, so that this man shall not at least boast to the public that these charges are so trifling that your Excellency will take no action upon them.

We have repeatedly contended for the enforcement of these laws. We have spent hundreds of dollars in the securing of evidence against these criminals. In due form of law we have brought the evidence of these crimes to the prosecuting attorney, there to meet with opposition; there to have our plans thwarted ; there to have complaints and indictments "pigeon-holed," while the offenders are permitted to openly violate the law.

On Friday afternoon, after having my interview with your Excellency, a young man came to my office and desired a confidential interview ; and in that interview he confessed that he was induced to visit the race track at Sheepshead Bay last June ; that he won a little at first, and that so sure was he of winning a fortune that he took money from his employer, expecting from his winnings to pay it back. He lost ; took more money ; continued to lose, and in his desperation, after taking about $2500, went to the wharf to throw himself into the river. Then he said : " I thought it was a cowardly thing to do. I thought of my wife and children, and I determined to go back and confess all," as he has done to his employers, who are now putting forth efforts to save him and help him redeem the past.

On Saturday there was arrested in Brooklyn, an employé of the well-known firm of Ovington Brothers, who confessed to Justice Walsh to stealing more than $1000 worth of silverware, knives, forks, etc., from the firm, and that he had spent the proceeds in the policy shop of Henry Dela Motta, of 308 Hudson Avenue ; the Henry Dela Motta being the one named in the charges before your Excellency as having been indicted June 14, 1883, but who has never been arraigned to plead to said indictment.

On Monday last a gentleman came to this office and asked for an interview with me, to get advice about a young man who had stolen his mother's watch and pawned it in a policy shop, in the city of New York. Before he was through he broke down and with tears streaming down his cheeks told me that it was his oldest boy, seventeen years of age.

Your Excellency, these are reasons why we contend for the enforcement of the law. These and similar cases, constantly coming to our notice, are the reasons why we appeal to you to secure the enforcement of the law against these crime-breeders in Kings County. ·

Gambling, like intemperance and lust, begets every other crime.

We respectfully submit that these charges should be considered, irrespective of whether there is an election about to take place, or whether there is a prospect or none of Mr. Ridgway's nomination. If nominated and elected, and then we come to you to press these charges, the plea will be made that the issue has been tried before the people of Kings County, and that they decided to re-elect this man.

It must be apparent to your Excellency that there can be no sifting of facts, and no proper investigation in the whirlpool of political strife preceding an election. One may say one thing, and another another. He says he is not guilty. We contend he is guilty, and we are ready to prove it to your Excellency.

Will not the Chief Executive of this State help this organization to secure such an enforcement of the law as shall save the weak ones in the community from these criminal disgraces, such as are constantly following in the wake of the reckless gambling thus permitted to be carried on in open violation of law?

His Honor, Judge Moore, in charging the Grand Jury, June 2, 1884, is reported by the papers as saying (concerning pool gambling in the town of Gravesend) : "The violations of the law are open, flagrant and persistent," and these words have been verified over and over again from that time down to the present time ; and yet, upon not one of all the large number of indictments found through the agency of this Society has a gambler been sentenced.

I have the honor to be,

On behalf of this society,

Your most obedient servant,

(Signed)　Anthony Comstock,

Secretary.

In November, 1886, Mr. Ridgway was re-elected. Prior to this, it will be remembered, the clergymen of Brooklyn had made an examination into the facts, concerning the charges made against Mr. Ridgway by the writer, and in the latter part of October they made an elaborate report (which was published in the Brooklyn papers), extracts of which are

.printed in the foregoing pages of this book. This report contains the following words :

" In conclusion the committee beg to say that after patient and laborious examination of the facts within their reach, together with the statements of interested parties, that they do not find that Mr. Comstock's statements can be successfully impeached in any essential particular.

The matter of the charges before Governor Hill dragged along until the 5th day of February, 1887, when Mr. Ridgway filed his answer before the Governor, *joining issue with the facts*, and then moved to dismiss on his answer. The very joining of issue, or denying the truth of the charges, raised a question of fact that could only be determined by evidence. If Mr. Ridgway had demurred to the charges, thus alleging that they were true, but did not constitute a ground for removal, then he might have had some basis for his motion to dismiss. But the moment he raised a question as to the truthfulness of the charges, then, according to all legal precedents, evidence as to the fact was next in order.

Governor Cleveland, in 1884, said of this case : " If Mr. Ridgway denies the facts, then the matter must be sent to a referee and evidence taken ; and if the charges are proven it is the solemn duty of the Chief Executive under his oath to remove Mr. Ridgway."

The decision of Governor Hill upon this motion of Mr. Ridgway to dismiss these charges, has not yet been rendered, so far as we can ascertain.

May 10, 1887, the report of the Bacon Investigating Committee was adopted by the Assembly at Albany. This report contained the following concerning Mr. Ridgway, which has a bearing upon the charges already filed before the Governor, to wit :

Upon the evidence before us it does not admit of doubt :
1. That Mr. Ridgway has systematically and deliberately protected

II

the persons violating the laws in Gravesend from prosecution; that out of such violations these persons have been earning great sums of money; that after warning them that he should prevent their violations and punish them if the offences were committed, nevertheless, for reasons which he does not explain, he immediately thereafter refrained from taking any steps whatever to make good his word.

2. That although vested by the law with the power to break up such gambling proceedings by a seizure of paraphernalia, he has refused to exercise the power.

3. That although numerous indictments have been found by Grand Juries during his term of office against individuals for gambling offences, he has deliberately and systematically contrived to prevent their cases being brought to trial.

4. That upon an indictment intended against John T. McDougall, and to which John T. McDougall pleaded, and upon which he gave bail, Mr. Ridgway knowingly tried a different person, with the intent to discredit the persons upon whose testimony John T. McDougall had been rightfully indicted, and to bring into disrepute the prosecution of such offenders.

5. That in the case of Paul Bauer, a well-known, wealthy, intelligent and important offender, who was Mr. Ridgway's personal client until he became District Attorney, Mr. Ridgway has, after a conviction, sentence, and affirmance of the conviction, permitted Bauer to go without serving his sentence, although there has been no stay of proceedings and no approval or acquiescence of the court.

6. That in order to prevent any proceedings against the Sheriff for his failure to proceed against gamblers, Mr. Ridgway, in October, 1886, advised the Grand Jury that a mere indictment of the Sheriff would remove him from office and cause a forfeiture of all his emoluments, although such was not the law, and although there was no reason to believe that such was the law.

These facts necessarily demonstrate that Mr. Ridgway should not be District Attorney of Kings County. The conclusion is so obvious that it does not need to be stated. Under our system prosecutions for crime depend upon the District Attorney. If he fail in the discharge of his duty, crime goes unpunished. The moment that it becomes understood that criminals may depend upon his indifference or partiality, restraint upon the commission of crime is weakened or withdrawn. The position of the District Attorney is unique. He is a law to himself. It is essential to the community that his discretion should be great; he is more largely trusted than any other officer of the law. But for this very reason the community must, for its mere safety, require from him the strictest loyalty to the intent of the law, and the most zealous and impartial discharge of his duty, when that duty is plain. If a judge commit error, the law provides a mode by which the error can be corrected. If an executive officer be bribed, the machinery of the government may still proceed. But all that is necessary to permit crime to be rampant is that a District Attorney, either by keeping cases from the Grand Jury or by ignoring the action of the Grand Jury when it is taken, shall omit to conduct the proceedings which are preliminary to the prosecution for crime and are essential to conviction. He is the adviser of the Grand Jury. He frames all indictments. No criminal can be brought to trial or successfully prosecuted without his instrumentality.

Under ordinary circumstances there would have been no embarrassment in determining what recommendation to make to meet Mr. Ridgway's case. He should be removed from office in the mode which has been prescribed and which has been heretofore followed. And although reasons may be suggested against this course at this time and in this case, the committee cannot see that they are called to recognize them or to deviate from the direct and ordinary course. It is true that Mr. Ridgway may be indicted. But if he is to be indicted it must be in the county of which he is himself District Attorney. That a District Attorney shall procure himself to be_indicted for violation of his duty as such cannot be expected. It may be said that Mr. Ridgway is liable to impeachment. That is true. But to have him tried by the Court of Impeachment will not only involve serious labor to the members of that court, will not only be attended with great expense, but, what is of much more consequence, will be to pursue an unusual and extraordinary course, the only reason for which would seem to be an unwillingness to leave his case with the Governor of the State.

We recommend that this report and the evidence upon which it is based be respectfully submitted to the Governor, that he may, in the usual method, proceed against James W. Ridgway, the District Attorney of Kings County, as the due administration of law and the welfare of the State require.

We waited till more than a year, in which by law they were entitled to appeal to the Court of Appeals, had passed, and no appeal having been filed in that court and not a gambler tried of our cases, we thought it best then to press these charges, which embraced a specification covering the failures of duty and violations of law as set out in this record.

What good has been accomplished by your appeals? may be asked.

The threat to go to the Governor, June 26, 1884, secured the indictment forthwith of twenty-two gamblers.

The appeal of the Executive Committee to Governor Cleveland, of Nov., 1884, forced the gamblers into court Dec. 1, 1884, and secured the eleven judgments of conviction.

The demand to the Grand Jury July, 1886, resulted in the indictment of the seventeen cases which Ridgway would not prosecute from Sept., 1884; and also the notice for gamblers to appear for sentence July 26, 1886.

The appeal made by us June, 1886, resulted in the sending of Mr. Shorter, the assistant District Attorney, down to Coney Island to notify the gamblers that they must cease their unlawful business, and temporarily it was done, while that Grand Jury was in session.

The filing of our charges, Sept. 10, 1886, was followed by the trial of two of the weakest cases we had, to wit : " The People *vs.* The Coney Island Jockey Club," and " The People *vs.* The Brighton Beach Racing Association," before that month was out.

By these gentle stimulants we have at least disturbed the " combine " and brought about what has been accomplished thus far.

We appealed to the Legislature, and an Investigating Committee has tested the truth of our charges.

This committee says of the New York Society for the Suppression of Vice as follows :—

It is proper here to refer to the public services rendered by the Society for the Suppression of Vice, and especially by its competent and vigorous agent, Anthony Comstock. Several of the witnesses before us, especially General Catlin and Mr. Ridgway, saw fit to attack Mr. Comstock. Mr. Ridgway did not hesitate to accuse him of blackmailing. But neither Mr. Ridgway nor General Catlin claimed to have personal knowledge of any fact inconsistent with Mr. Comstock's integrity of purpose. It appeared that their dislike of him had arisen solely from his persistent and unceasing efforts to have them perform their duties in the prosecution of gamblers. It was insinuated that there might be difficulty in procuring convictions upon Mr. Comstock's evidence; but as to this there was no more than insinuation. No reference was made to any case in which a jury had disbelieved the testimony either of Mr. Comstock or of his subordinates. On the contrary, Mr. Backus, General Catlin's first assistant, and to whom was committed the actual trial of the gambling cases, testified (p. 977) that down to the expiration of his term of office Mr. Comstock was "continually crowding these prosecutions" against the gamblers; that without subpœnas he produced the witnesses; that he "was always ready and came freely and always testified promptly; he and his men were always there on time in all of the lottery policy cases;" that conviction always resulted in the cases that were prosecuted by Mr. Comstock and his men and which were tried; that he "never lost a case with Mr. Comstock as a witness—Mr. Comstock and his men." It is impossible that the services to the public of the nature of those performed by Mr. Comstock should not be attended with a pertinacity extremely disagreeable to those counter to whose wishes or interests Mr. Comstock has gone. Work such as Mr. Comstock performs is vitally essential to the safety and decency of the community. But few citizens are willing to make the sacrifice necessary to its performance. From the testimony before us, we are convinced that the community owes Mr. Comstock and his Society a very great debt; that there is no reason to doubt their entire sincerity and honesty of purpose; that the intelligence with which their work is performed is of a high order, and that it simply needs proper official co-operation to secure a wholesome success most valuable to the cause of public morals.

Now, at last, we appeal to the public and present the facts for their consideration.

Have we proven worthy of the confidence and favor of good citizens? We have not gained the favor of the gamblers nor their friends. We have not sought that. Have we earned a right to be heard? Are not these facts worthy of honest contemplation?

Read some of the *special arguments* for this new gambling system of "improving the breed of horses."

CHAPTER X.

SPECIAL ARGUMENTS.

THE following cases are respectfully submitted to thought-ful men for their consideration. They are specially com-mended to the advocates of gambling in any form.

This chapter contains the harvest of the gamblers. We point to the following cases as the strongest arguments why the law should be enforced and why gamblers should be hurled from power.

These arguments are particularly commended to the at-tention of the " eminent gentlemen of wealth and position" who have petitioned the Legislature to "improve the breed of horses " at the expense of the morals of the community.

A former town treasurer of Union, N. J., arrested for the defalcation of about $3200, confessed to having taken and lost it in Barclay Street pool rooms.

A former clerk of the New York Ferry Company stole $2800 before being detected, which he also lost in the same manner.

A father, a former member of the Legislature of the State of New York, called at our office, saying his son, while at college, had stolen his mother's watch and pawned the same to raise $100 to gamble with.

George Dorrance was arrested for stealing $1500, which he lost in Hunters Point pool rooms.

A trusted clerk in a large mercantile house on Broadway, New York, in a few weeks' time managed to embezzle over $10,000 from his employer to gamble with. This case was brought to our notice by the employers of this thief, who sought our aid and assistance in the matter.

Another clerk of a Broadway bank confessed to stealing over $33,400, all of which he spent in gambling.

In Orange, N. J., a bright young man committed suicide, leaving as a parting message to his friends, "An unconquerable habit of gambling has rendered life intolerable."

A few months ago at Newark, N. J., a youth pleaded "guilty of murder in the second degree," for killing a friend at the gambling table.

A young man formerly employed by Fussell & Co. was brought to our office in New York, and confessed to stealing over $1800 in small sums from his employers to gamble with.

A young man was sentenced by Recorder Smyth, in New York, to two and one-half years' imprisonment for stealing $175 worth of jewelry. His plea was, " I have imbibed a taste for gambling."

A treasurer of a church, crazed by gambling schemes, embezzled $1400 of a trust fund to gamble with.

One Saurbraum lost $500 in the Coney Island pool rooms, July, 1883, of moneys not belonging to himself.

A cashier in a banking house in Pine Street claims to have lost $30,000 of his employers' money in gambling.

Michael McKensie, age seventeen, embezzled $133, which he lost betting on the races at Brighton Beach last summer.

A clerk, of 23 Maiden Lane, upon being arrested for stealing three gold watches in March last, when asked by the court, " What made you do this?" replied: "I bought pools on horse races and became heavily in debt."

April 11, 1885, a mother writes to the Brooklyn *Eagle* as follows :

"I have two sons. One of them occupied a good position in a large house in New York, where he earned a large salary. He commenced buying pools on horses so that the influence and excitement of it caused him to neglect his business and in a short time leave his position altogether. The other son is fast following in his footsteps, and God only knows where they will turn up. I state these facts to show what trials and heart-aches a great many mothers have to endure after bringing up their boys to manhood, only to see them ruined through betting on horses, and I only hope that the time is not far distant when pool-selling will be abolished."

In the Brooklyn *Union*, June 5, 1885, we find that T. H. Halstead, a boy, stole $85 from a trunk belonging to a clerk in a grocery store and went to the Jerome Park races to spend it, where he was apprehended.

The Brooklyn *Eagle*, July 16, 1885, records that Thomas A. Broughton yesterday broke open his grandmother-in-law's trunk and stole $355 in gold to go and see the races.

In the New York *World*, September 3, 1885, we find that M. Floury, an official, having been detected of embezzling public funds, committed suicide. He was led to steal by his heavy losses at gambling.

Says the Brooklyn *Union*, Sept. 13, 1885: "A once prosperous Greenpoint merchant goes to the dogs by reason of attending horse races and pool playing. A once prominent merchant has been turned out of the house by his wife and made to shift for himself. She said she had given her husband but a short time previous $200 to go away and never return ; but he followed his old habit of attending horse races and pool rooms. He soon lost the amount and came back for more."

In the Brooklyn *Union*, Oct. 4, 1885, we find the following item :

"RUINED BY BETTING.—Gambling and horse races ruin an Admiral's son. How William H. Cooper got into trouble. A model young man until he began backing the races. Loses $8000 on one race. He was charged with having obtained $3000 under false pretences."

New York *Tribune*, Oct. 8, 1885.—John Fuller loses $5000 at gambling.

New York *Sun*, Nov. 16, 1885.—Thomas D. Wright, a young man, loses $90 at gambling.

New York *Sun*, Jan. 4, 1886.—Young Frederick Fiskel, this city, stole $75,000, which he spent in gambling at the races.

Morning Journal, Feb. 18, 1886.—Edward Davison ruined by gambling. Neglects to support his family and pawns everything that he can lay his hands on to get money to spend in gambling. Last week he took his overcoat from his back and pawned it to get money to gamble with. His wife drew $17 from the bank, that had been placed there for her boy, to pay her rent with.

Brooklyn *Eagle*, July 1, 1886.—Harry Wheeler, an agent of the Long Island Railroad Co., lost $500 at gambling. An investigation of Wheeler's accounts revealed that he was about $500 short, and he would have been arrested had not his father promptly made good the deficiency.

In the Brooklyn *Standard* of July 2, 1886, we find that Robert J. Blood, New York, a collector, attempted to commit suicide last night by shooting himself. On Tuesday Blood lost $400 by gambling on Miss Woodford, and this money had been collected from the customers of Evans and had not been turned over or an accounting given of it. A cursory examination of the books has been made. It is believed that the collector embezzled something like $200. It is thought that the wounded man cannot live. He had a wife and children.

Again in Brooklyn *Standard*, July 22, 1886.—Joseph Fogarty, a lad 16 years of age, forges checks and is another victim of pool-selling at Coney Island.

A long account in the New York *World*, Aug. 31, 1886, discloses that L. Symons has kept a butcher store in the city of Brooklyn for more than twenty years. A month ago he disappeared, leaving, as it has since been found, a long list of creditors. It is believed that Symons committed suicide, as nothing has been heard from him. The total losses gone to the pool-sellers, it is said, will reach nearly $80,000.

Still later in the Brooklyn *Standard*, Oct. 11, 1886. —Ruined by gambling. When Henry Brown, a watchman in the employ of Ovington Brothers, was arrested upon a charge of grand larceny, he confessed his guilt and said that the money he derived from the sale of the goods was invested by him in the policy shop of Henry Dela Motta.

Brooklyn *Standard*, Oct. 18, 1886.—A victim of the gamblers. A. M. Pinkley was found dead in bed yesterday at the Henderson House, where he had been staying for a week. On the Friday before he had lost $180 at the races.

From the New York *World*, May 8, 1886, we take the following:

" Mrs. Hale, a young woman who is not married six months, entered Recorder Schleicher's court in Union Hill yesterday morning. She said that she had only been married six months, and had lived happily until her husband began to squander his money on races and then came home and abused her. He had left home, and after three days' searching for him she found him in the house of a disreputable woman in North Bergen."

The New York *Tribune* of Dec. 27, 1886, contained the following editorial on the sad suicide of a young man who became desperate from his losses betting upon horse races :

" That was a pitiful cry which the suicide from a Brooklyn ferryboat sent from his watery grave on Christmas eve—' Keep away from horse-racing and pool-rooms.' It was not in harmony with the spirit of the joyous Christmas-tide, but there is a lesson here worth heeding, a sermon more impressive, doubtless, than many preached yesterday in our pulpits."

In October last a bright young man of about twenty-eight years of age, having a wife and three small children, called at our office and desired an interview with the writer. After a little he confessed to having stolen more than $2500 from his employer. His story, briefly told, was to the effect that in June last he visited the Coney Island Jockey Club race course and made a bet with some of the gamblers. Unfortunately he won a small sum. This seemed to turn his head. He conceived the idea that he could speedily make a fortune. He used all his own savings and then, to use his own words, "borrowed from the money drawer of his employer." Again he lost and again "borrowed" to help make good his losses. From the race course he was led to "Big Mike" Murray's gambling saloon in New York, where in one night he lost over $1000. All this while he was lured on by the gambler's false beacon that "my luck will soon turn," until, becoming desperate from his failures to win, unable to meet his deficiencies, with a horror of disgrace and exposure, in a desperate moment he went down to the wharf in Brooklyn one night to commit suicide. He said: "I thought of my wife and children, and of the additional disgrace to come upon them, and I determined for their sakes to be a man, confess all, and suffer the consequences."

The same week a father, a general salesman, who was associated in a large wholesale dry-goods house years ago with me, called, seeking my advice concerning a young lad seventeen years of age who had stolen his mother's gold watch to pawn to get money to gamble with. Bursting into tears, he afterwards acknowledged the young man to be his oldest son.

How many cases, equally as sad and appalling, are constantly coming to light!

Must these facts go for naught? Is there not an unanswerable argument in these wrecked lives? What of the home circle? What has the mother, or the wife and innocent, helpless children, in the homes of the victims of these gambling passions done, that their hearts must thus be

pierced with agony no tongue can tell and their heads
bowed with shame and mortification over the downfall of
their loved ones ?

Is there not something in this county and State of more
account than horse-flesh, especially when the improvement
of the stock costs such a price ?   Yet respectable men, men
of wealth and position, composing these jockey clubs, are
ready to advocate the system, even in the face of such
horrors, and cheerfully divide blood-money with these
gambling harpies !   .

Other interesting facts concerning secret manipulations are
constantly coming to the surface, illustrating how unscrupulous men manipulate the very contingency upon which
the pool is sold or the bet made.   The gambler secretly
manipulates, while the public blindly invest their money upon
the contingency he is operating.

June 29, 1884, the Brooklyn *Union*, in reporting a race at
Sheepshead Bay the previous afternoon, says, in speaking of
the defeat of a horse named " Eole " :

" Eole was in superb condition and ran nobly.   Most of those who
stood in full view of the finish hailed Eole as the winner.   Indeed, it
looked beyond doubt that the horse would win.   But it seemed as if his
jockey did not intend that he should win.   Instead of keeping to his
work, he made no effort to urge the animal forward, and by sheer
negligence lost the race.   Mr. Walton had placed his thousands on
Eole, and before this race considered his jockey, Donohue, second to
none in this country.   Men who ought to know said that the book-
makers were up to their dirty work again.   It was openly stated on the
course that Donohue had been bought up by the gamblers.   The result
of the book-jack Eole race disgusted even the most tolerant with the
book-making fraternity, and proved beyond question how disastrous to
true sport is their presence at the track."

From the New York *World* we find as follows :

" Yesterday was the last day of the autumn meeting of Jerome Park,
and large fields and good racing, with their inevitable accompaniment
of heavy betting, were the result.   Horses from all over the country

were entered in the handicap sweepstakes, purses, and steeplechase that made up the programme of six events. From what could be learned last night the fraud perpetrated was the most gigantic ever known."

It will be recalled that a few years ago a scene occurred at the Monmouth Park race track between Francis T. Walton and James E. Kelly, "boss" gambler. Mr. Walton, better known as the "American Plunger" on the English race courses, was the proprietor of the St. James Hotel and contracted for the cleaning of the streets of New York south of 14th Street. According to the *Tribune* of July 28, 1882, "Mr. Kelly declared that Mr. Walton had Marathon 'pulled' in the race with Hospodar on Thursday of last week. Mr. Kelly further accused the Plunger of dishonest practices, saying he bought up the owners of horses as well as the trainers and jockeys, and was responsible for bringing American racing into disgrace."

In the discussion that followed in the public press some of the tactics possible on the race track were discussed. In describing some of these the *Tribune* further says (in speaking of a certain man) that "on the day before the race he would quietly visit the owners of each of the horses entered for a certain event and would ask each what he thought of his horse's chances of winning; and when he discovered the most confident owner, would say to him, 'I'll bet you $1000 to nothing that your horse does not win the race.' The purse offered would perhaps be only $300 or $500, and the owner would see the wisdom of forcing his horse to win even if he was compelled to 'stiffen' the other horses entered for the race. Then this man would go to the jockey and would say to him, 'Do you think you can win the race?' Should the jockey reply in the affirmative, he would say, 'I bet you $500 to nothing that you do not.' That would be enough to make the jockey risk his life in attempting to win it."

Then the testimony of the book-maker is given, which says that "horses were 'stiffened' up, that is, filled with water or fodder just before the race, so as to throw them out of condition."

Later, when this matter was brought up for action before the Jockey Club, it was announced in the *Herald* that there were "counter charges," and there were a number of cases cited where horses were "pulled" to enable another horse to win, and where attempts had been made at such arrangements and had failed.

It was alleged at this time that as high as one thousand dollars had been paid to induce the jockey to "pull" the horse, and that jockeys were brought in who swore that they had been paid to "pull" the horses, and further, that the "boss" gambler himself had been guilty of the same charges that he claimed "The Plunger" was guilty of.

Without attempting to pass upon the truth or falsity of these charges made at that time, and simply referring to them for illustrations, it will still be seen that there is suspicion in the minds of even the book-makers, and that they have to guard one against the other. While they are thus looking out for their own interests, what becomes of the interests of the great public who know nothing of what is going on behind the scenes and whose property is at the mercy of these schemers?

Frequent statements have been published by the press that telegraph wires have been tapped, private wires connected with gambling dens in New York and elsewhere, so that gamblers could thus be advised in advance so as to take advantage of their customers. For instance, at French pool the holders of tickets upon the winning horse receive the pool, less a percentage to the boss gambler. Being advised beforehand of the results of the race, the "boss" sends his stool-pigeons to purchase tickets upon the winning horse, and thus defrauds the holders of winning tickets in just proportion to the number of tickets he buys of his own men at the booths. This scheme is worked away from the race course by pool gamblers—placed where returns are received by telegraph.

These are some of the inducements offered to the public by the gambling fraternity. These are the scientific methods of " improving the breed of horses."

CHAPTER XI.

SARATOGA.

AT Saratoga Springs gambling is not called "improving the breed of horses." Gambling of all kinds is tolerated there because, it is claimed, it would "ruin Saratoga," and "all of the big hotels would have to close," if the law against professional gamblers should be enforced.

WHO ARE THE GAMBLERS THAT ARE THE LIFE OF SARATOGA?

Who are these mighty men of valor that support upon their shoulders the town of Saratoga Springs, with all its best interests? Who are the celebrities whose attractions are so powerful and the support which they render the town of Saratoga so great that in comparison with which its health-giving springs go for naught?

It may well be asked: "What is the little town of Saratoga Springs, with all its interests, compared to the proper administration of law and justice in the Empire State?"

Last summer at Saratoga there were professional gamblers from Ohio, Kentucky, Michigan, Delaware, Maryland, New Jersey, Pennsylvania, while others were from the city of New York—non-residents of the town of Saratoga Springs. These non-residents of the State of New York stood side by side with local officials—Deputy Sheriffs and Constables—all engaged in violating the law. While these non-residents and official gamblers were thus violating the law, other peace officers, with the insignias of their office upon them, stood where they could witness and know the facts and permitted the laws of the State to be openly trampled under foot.

Warning after warning came to our office that any attempt to enforce the law at Saratoga would be met with bloody resistance. Information was brought to us that gamblers were not only there from other States, but that numerous lawless characters had been drawn to Saratoga by these gambling opportunities, and that it would be easy to have some of these strangers assault the agents of this Society and then escape, as there would be no interference on the part of local authorities; and if there was, the gambling spirit was so strong, and their control over the officials so complete, that nothing would be done with the assassin. A case where the proprietors of one of these gambling saloons had deliberately shot down a man on the public street and then escaped, together with another case where a man was hacked to pieces in front of one of the large hotels by a mob of gamblers, was cited to show the absolute recklessness of these men and the lawless condition of that town. These were presented as " awful examples "—reasons for us not to proceed.

In July, 1886, an appeal was made by some of the better class of citizens of Saratoga to this Society for us to move against these crimes. The last week of July the writer, accompanied by Mr. M. J. Sullivan, one of his assistants, visited Saratoga in person. As it afterwards turned out, the fact that we had gone to Saratoga was telegraphed from Albany by some person unbeknown to us, and the papers the next morning announced our presence. We knew that whatever was done must be done secretly and at once. After securing lodgings in a private house, as soon as it became dark, the night of our arrival, the writer went to a barber, shaved off his side whiskers, which he had worn for years, dressed himself in light apparel, and went, not only into the headquarters of the Saratoga Racing Association, near the Club House on Putnam Street, but also into the Club House itself, kept by Albert Spencer and Charles Reed. This was known as the "John Morrissey gambling den." The

12

doors open freely to the public, one opening from Putnam Street and one from East Congress Street. In one
room were no less than three double roulette wheels and layouts and four other banking games, including faro and other
games—all in full operation.

At the headquarters of the Racing Association "auction
pools" and "combination pools" were sold in full view, with
windows and doors opening to the street, so that even pass-
ers-by could see and hear all that was going on. This place
was each night thronged with people gathered there to gamble. We secured the evidence against the parties in these
two places before we slept the first night.

The next morning, changing our apparel again, we went
out to the race course, and there found fifteen or sixteen
gambling booths where the firm name or the name of the
gambler was displayed at the head of a blackboard upon
which were the names of the horses of each race, with the
odds the gambler was giving against each horse. In front of
each of these booths stood the boss gambler, calling out the
odds he was giving and bidding for trade. To the left of
the grand stand was a little plot or pavilion fenced off with
an iron fence, and under this tent or pavilion were these
gambling booths. On the fence was a sign, "BETTING
RING." Just inside of the gate through this fence stood a
detective-sergeant on guard who belongs at police headquarters in the city of New York, a man well known about this
city. Directly back of where he stood was a "French pool"
box where a deputy sheriff was the principal seller and a local constable his assistant, who recorded the bets. At another stand another one of the constables of Saratoga County,
with his assistant, ran another "French pool" box. Then
following the circle further around were men from Detroit,
Cincinnati, Louisville, and New York city, and other places.
In and out were peace officers with their insignias of office
upon them.

We secured the evidence against fifteen of the principal gamblers at this place. We then went back to our rooms, and after dinner took a stroll on Broadway, going into 402 Broadway, which was next door to the District Attorney's office, where we found three men engaged as pool gamblers ; a roulette layout was in full operation, while in a room adjoining were two faro banks, one of them in full blast. Here we found policemen in uniform with their badges of office upon them, while out of the faro bank windows we could look into the District Attorney's office.

Within twenty-four hours after reaching Saratoga we had obtained the evidence against twenty-nine gamblers. Thinking it wise policy to defer any further investigations till the next day, and in order that we might more carefully write out a description of the men and our dealings with them and what we had witnessed, we kept our rooms.

The next morning we were waited upon by friends and advised to leave town. Threat was brought to us that "if we remained our body would be sent home in a box " and " our blood spilled upon the streets of Saratoga."

Trusting in the all-powerful One as our shield and defence, we determined to remain and do our duty at all hazards. It seemed, however, wise for us to prepare the papers and complaints in the cases where we had the evidence. This required nearly all of Wednesday and Thursday. Other threats came in with words of warning, and so great was the excitement that we were not able to get further evidence at that time. So fierce was the opposition that we were boycotted by hackmen, while threats were heard on every side. Then a delay seemed necessary in order that we might have a public meeting to counteract the sentiment against law and order.

The pastors of the churches met together, and it was resolved to hold a public meeting. This meeting was held on the third of August, 1886. Rev. Herrick Johnson, D.D., of

Chicago, presided.   Rev. Joseph Cook, Rev. W. F. Terrett, of Saratoga Springs, and others spoke.   The following gentlemen were Vice-Presidents, all of whom, I believe, gave their consent to the use of their names for this meeting, to wit: Hon. Henry Hilton, Spencer Trask, Alanson B. Trask, John W. Ehninger, Dr. R. C. McEwen, E. W. Fuller, Dr. R. Hamilton, W. A. Shepard, Dr. S. J. Pearsall, Prof. H. A. Wilson, E. C. Clark, S. A. Richard, L. W. James, Rev. C. F. Dowd, Charles S. Smith, E. R. Atterbury, W. H. Mc-Caffrey, Rev. Dr. J. B. Smith, Prof. G. W. Yates, Rev. Dr. James Brophy, Bishop Foster, Rev. Dr. J. L. Withrow, Rev. T. W. Jones, Rev. W. R. Terrett, Rev. R. F. McMichael, Dr. S. V. Leach, Rev. Z. Osborne, Rev. C. J. Young, Prof. E. M. Jones, Dr. T. B. Reynolds, Rev. A. Proudfit, Rev. J. N. Crocker, Rev. John McMenomy, Rev. Joseph Carey.

Again the writer was warned not to attend this meeting, under threats of assault, if not of assassination, Relying upon the Divine hand for guidance and direction, we went to this meeting, which was held in the Baptist church in Washington Street.   It was said that at least 100 gamblers were present.   The writer was met almost as soon as he came out of his rooms and followed to the door of the church by certain parties who boasted that it was their intention of assaulting him.   Among the number were the deputy-sheriff gambler and a town policeman, the latter being the aggressor and ringleader.

Passing over the excitement and dangers of that hour, suffice it to say that the meeting was a grand success, and, under Providence, made it possible for the agents of this Society to remain in Saratoga, and on the fourth, fifth, and sixth days of August following this meeting to arrest twenty-three of the twenty-nine gamblers against whom we had evidence and complaints.   We raided the Club House, and seized the three double roulette tables and one gaming table, the others having been removed before the officer reached the place.

No. 402 Broadway was closed effectually for the time being, all of the gambling paraphernalia having been removed.

It was reported that the day we placed our complaints in the hands of the District Attorney no less than twenty-eight gambling saloons closed their places and moved away their paraphernalia. Certain it was that in places where roulette wheels and layouts and faro banks were run in full blast when we first went to Saratoga, these games closed temporarily.

No person not acquainted with the facts can form any conception of the absolute control the gamblers have over Saratoga. Citizens, merchants, hotel keepers, and others were afraid of being boycotted if they attempted to interfere or lend their influence against this gambling fraternity.

August 4, 1886, the complaints were laid before Mr. Justice Barbour, of Saratoga, who not only promptly issued his warrants, but rendered every assistance and protection to the agents aforesaid. He did his duty bravely and is deserving of much praise.

Strange as it may seem, however, when these gamblers were notified of our complaints against them, like Captain Scott's coon, each one of them "came down without a shot being fired," came voluntarily into court, waived examination, and gave bail to await the action of the Grand Jury.

The question naturally arises, What guarantee, if any, had been given by the local authorities that insured this docility on their part? That the District Attorney and local authorities knew of the open violation of law they will not deny, nor would any person who visited Saratoga believe them if they did deny it; for these gambling games were carried on so openly that the fact was patent to every one.

But notwithstanding the fact that there was positive evidence secured, and that the gamblers were apprehended and held in bail to await the action of the Grand Jury, the Grand Jury which met in October last at Ballston, N. Y., in

the Oyer and Terminer Court, over which his Honor Judge
Potter presided, ignored the most positive evidence presented
to them, which evidence was written down by the District
Attorney. Not a bill of indictment was found against a
single one of these twenty-three gamblers. Indeed, we
brought into court witnesses other than our own witnesses,
and in some instances at least five witnesses were examined;
yet notwithstanding all this, there could not be found enough
men on that Grand Jury who regarded their oaths sufficiently
to order a bill of indictment. The evidence of guilt was
firmly sustained against the gamblers, *and was not contradicted*, and in some instances the violations of law were known
to some of the members of that Grand Inquest.

Let it be remembered that the " keeping of a room,
paraphernalia, or place for gambling purposes " is indictable,
and that in each of these cases the crimes complained` of
were committed so publicly that any person could have seen
and known that they were being committed. They were
committed *openly*, and every act of the gamblers was open
to public view. Yet with that fact brought to the attention
of that Grand Jury, these men were willing to go on record
as *ignoring* the *evidence*, regardless of their oath, by which
they were bound to find according to the evidence and the
law. I speak thus positively because I know personally of
the absolute character of the evidence submitted.

The following were members of that Grand Jury, as published in the *Saratogian*, September 23, 1886 :

Charlton.—Charles Haines and Edward Merchant.

Clifton Park.—Alexander T. Knowlton.

Edinburgh.—Samuel A. Brownell.

Half Moon.—Daniel Dunham.

Milton.—Thomas D. Colson, John Richards, E. F. Grose,
Isaac K. Grennell, and Sylvester S. Gould.

Malta.—Walton Haight.

Saratoga Springs.—Lewis Wood, Sidney A. Rickard, J. H.

Walbridge, James McLaughlin, Lewis Wagman, and Charles D. Thurber.

Saratoga.—George Clark, Amos Salsbury, and DeWitt Thomas.

Wilton.—Jesse B. Thorn.

Waterford.—James Byrnes and Charles E. Devitt.

NATURE OF EVIDENCE THEY IGNORED.

Our complaints contained two counts. One affidavit formally charged the statutory offence, while the second was really a formal examination of the witness.

In this connection it will be of interest to observe the oath as prescribed by law, under Section 245 of the Code of Criminal Procedure, of the Grand Jury, to wit :

" You, as foreman of this Grand Jury, shall diligently inquire and true presentment make of all such matters and things as shall be given you in charge; the counsel of the people of this State, your fellows', and your own you shall keep secret; you shall present no person from envy, hatred, or malice ; *nor shall you leave any one unpresented through fear, favor, affection, or reward, or hope thereof ; but you shall present all things truly as they come to your knowledge*, according to the best of your ability. So help you God."

Section 246 provides the following for each member of the Grand Jury. After the foreman has been sworn, the balance are sworn as follows :

" The same oath which your foreman has now taken before you on his part, you and each of you shall well and truly observe on your part. So help you God."

In order that the public may be informed of the nature of the evidence against these criminals, I desire to present a specimen of the evidence we obtained against some of these men. For instance : at the Club House there were two men at one roulette table, dealing (who were positively identified), and the game of roulette was being played, bets were being made by players and money lost. The witnesses saw the paraphernalia, saw the game dealt, saw the money paid by the players, saw them receive money when they won and pay in their chips when they lost. Of faro the same is true at the same place.

At 402 Broadway, first floor, directly off the street was a saloon, in the first room back of which two men were selling pools. In order to show exactly what they did, we purchased pools of these men and produced them in evidence against them. The pool, in each case, was recorded by them upon a book in our presence, and also upon a paper which they handed to us. In the next room adjoining was a roulette table and layout in full blast, where players were losing their money, almost as fast as they paid it out for chips. Within a few feet of this was a faro bank, where we also saw game after game played, saw money lost and won, and saw the paraphernalia kept and used by these men in violation of the law. The dealers and lookout were all positively identified.

At the race track we purchased a pool ticket of a Deputy Sheriff, he received the money for it, and his assistant, the Constable, recorded it. This pool ticket happened to be a winner. In order to more plainly establish the evidence and the transaction, we made a copy of the ticket and cashed it in, and then bought another one, so as to be sure to show the transaction. We kept the money as an exhibit in the case. This all was taken before the Grand Jury. We also saw the paraphernalia, the "French pool" instrument used in recording these bets, all of which and any of which is, in itself, sufficient to have indicted these men.

The Secretary of the Grand Jury, Mr. Walbridge, said to the writer: "What will be the expense of trying these men if we indict them?" The writer replied that he respectfully submitted he had no right to consider that question in the matter of the guilt or innocence of these men. This man then said that he "was a tax-payer in the town of Saratoga, and that he should consider that question." He doubt-less did consider this or some other question rather than the evidence that was submitted by witnesses who were uncon-tradicted.

The next Grand Jury for that county met January, 1887. In the mean time the term of Mr. John Foley, who was then District Attorney, having expired, he was succeeded by Mr. Hamilton, the new District Attorney, who came into office January 1, 1887. In order that Mr. Hamilton might be in-formed of the facts, the letter presented below was sent to him with the request, as will be seen, that these cases be brought before the Grand Jury.　　　　　　　．

We maintain that our correspondence faithfully brings home upon officials a knowledge of the facts, and places the responsibility of non-enforcement of law against gambling upon them.

It may be a technical excuse that the Grand Jury did not indict these gamblers in October last, but that would in no wise justify such reckless indifference to the flagrant, per-sistent, and open violations of law. "It is the duty of all District Attorneys to inform against and prosecute all per-sons whom he has reason to believe offenders against these laws." So says Section 349, Penal Code.

In order to prevent the bonds of these gamblers from being dismissed and to bring them before another court, the following letter was sent the presiding Judge :

October 7, 1886.

Hon. Judge POTTER,
　　　　Ballston, N. Y.

Dear Sir:—It is announced in the morning papers here that the Grand Jury in the court over which you have the honor to preside failed to find bills of indictment against those persons charged with violating gambling laws.

I respectfully present to your Honor that the evidence against the twenty-seven persons complained of by myself and Michael J. Sullivan is of the most positive character, and the proof before the Grand Jury is

ABSOLUTE IN ITS NATURE.   The minutes taken in writing by the District Attorney will confirm what I say.

From statements made to me by a member of the Grand Jury, and also statements made by Mr. Wallbridge, the Secretary, I am positive, and am informed and verily believe, that the jury have allowed considerations other than law and evidence to control their actions.   Mr. Wallbridge, the Secretary, said in my presence, to and in presence of the Grand Jury, that if the Grand Jury indicted these men it would cost the county $50,000.   I said : " You as a Grand Juror have nothing to do with this.   You are not allowed to consider this in connection with these cases.   You are sworn to find according to law and evidence."   He replied before the Grand Jury that he should consider that matter in the consideration of these cases, and I submit to your Honor that for this jury to ignore the absolute and positive evidence as laid before them is a reckless disregard of their oaths, in contempt of law and your Honor's charge, and against the welfare of this community.   It is a revolutionary and dangerous proceeding.   I earnestly appeal to your Honor to sustain the right.   Will you not examine the record, and as some of these men are ignorant and unused to court matters, charge them as to their duty ? They have nothing to do with the cost of trying these cases or the deciding of the evidence of guilt.   Wallbridge said : " I am a large tax-payer, and I tell you I shall consider this "—the cost of prosecution.

These gamblers openly defied and violated the law and continued so to do after arrest, as I am informed and verily believe.   They boasted that they controlled matters, that nothing could be or would be done.   If the rumors of the dismissal of these cases be true, then, I respectfully submit, I am more than justified in appealing to your Honor to take this jury in hand and make them understand and do their duty under their oaths as jurors.   Otherwise the reproach of outraged law and their boast of their being able to control courts and juries must continue.   I am sure your Honor will understand the outrage upon justice, when you examine the evidence we laid before this jury.

If desirable, I will gladly come to the court and make any affidavit required to further the ends of justice.

I have the honor to be, with very great respect, dear sir,

Your obedient servant,

(Signed) ANTHONY COMSTOCK.

I am informed by Mr. Foley, then District Attorney, that the bail-bonds against these gamblers continued in force.

The plea of " cost of prosecution " is a most absurd and

specious one. The Court and District Attorney exist, and are paid whether the gamblers are tried or not. The law and the evidence were very clear. A conviction in these cases would have enabled the court to impose a fine which would more than cover the costs of prosecution. The following letter was sent to the new District Attorney:

NEW YORK, *December* 7, 1886.

Hon. T. L. HAMILTON,
        District Attorney,
            Saratoga County, N. Y.

Dear Sir:—I beg to call your attention to the following cases, to wit:

    People *vs.* Charles A. Cook,
      "   " J. F. Waring,
      "   " Edward J. Beaman,
      "   " John H. White,
      "   " John Lee,
      "   " John S. Davis,
      "   " John Fryer,
      "   " James Minnick,
      "   " Leo Meyer,
      "   " James Gallagher,
      "   " J. F. Finn,
      "   " William M. Carroll,
      "   " Joseph Cotton,
      "   " Peter Knight,
      "   " Geo. Bowman,
      "   " Henry Davis,
      "   " Christian W. Schaffer,
      "   " Michael J. Cummings,
      "   " Alex. J. Clarke,
      "   " Geo. J. Viall,
      "   " Jas. H. Vanderbergh,
      "   " Edwin McGoughan,
      "   " Chas. W. Medinger.

As you are doubtless aware, gambling has been openly carried on in the County of Saratoga for years. I am informed by an attorney who resides part of the year in Saratoga Springs that you have been elected as District Attorney, on the anti-gambling platform, and that it is your determination to enforce the laws of the State against any who violate the same.

I need not say to you that every honest citizen hails this with delight ; and I desire to extend to you my most cordial and hearty co-operation in what I have no doubt you will find, in many respects, a very difficult task.

The foregoing parties were arrested and held for the action of the Grand Jury last summer. They were brought before the October Grand Jury, and notwithstanding the most positive and absolute evidence of guilt presented and uncontradicted, the Grand Jury failed to indict a single one.

In order that you may be fully prepared in these cases, I have simply to call your attention to the complaints, which set out fully and specifically the offences which each party is charged with. I would further ask your consideration to the minutes of the Grand Jury, which are written out fully in each case.

One of the Grand Jurors said to me in substance as follows : that if these parties were indicted, it would add to the tax list of the county to secure their trial and conviction, and that that was a consideration which would influence him in his findings as a Grand Juror. I protested then and there, and went to the presiding Judge with the statements thus made, and I am advised that there were considerations other than that of the Judge's charge or the sworn testimony of the witnesses which led the Grand Jury to fail to indict the parties complained of. In view of these facts, I asked the then District Attorney, Mr. Foley, and the presiding Judge not to permit the bonds to be dismissed, and I was informed that all the cases were to be sent to the next Grand Jury.

I am informed that the court which meets in January will be the next Grand Jury; and I respectfully ask that all of the cases may be brought before the coming Grand Jury, and that the witnesses who were examined before the last Grand Jury may be called and further examined in the premises. The minutes of the Grand Jury will furnish you the names of the witnesses in the case of Spencer & Reed, proprietors of the Club House, and also proprietors of the race track. Also the witnesses in the case of Cale Mitchell, the proprietor of the other gambling establishment raided upon Broadway, Saratoga. Mr. M. J. Sullivan and myself are the witnesses in all these cases, and we will accept service of subpœna through the mail and be on hand subject to your orders.

As I have other matters to look after, I would respectfully ask that you will give us a few days' notice, so that I can arrange my other cases that I happen to have in any other courts.

I beg to say to you that you may be assured of the heartiest co-opera-

•

tion on the part of this office in reference to these or any other cases that may come up during your administration.

> I have the honor to be,
> With very great respect, sir,
> Your obedient servant,
> (Signed) ANTHONY COMSTOCK,
> Secretary.

To insure success, that there should be no lack of knowledge on the part of the Court, the following letter was also sent to Hon. Charles O. Tappan, Potsdam, N. Y., the judge who was to preside at the Court of Oyer and Terminer, at Ballston, N. Y., at the next term in January, to wit :

(Dictated.)

NEW YORK, *December* 7, 1886.

Hon. CHARLES O. TAPPAN,
Potsdam, N. Y.

Dear Sir :—

Having been informed that you are to preside at the court in Saratoga County, and will have charge of the Grand Jury in the month of January, 1887, I beg most respectfully to present, on behalf of the law-abiding citizens of that county, and also on behalf of this Society, that for years gambling has been openly carried on in Saratoga County at Saratoga Springs, in defiance of Sections 344 and 351 of the Penal Code.

Notwithstanding that Section 344 makes the keeping of a room and apparatus for gambling a felony, two men, Reed & Spencer, kept a Club House at Saratoga where the banking games of faro, roulette, etc., were openly carried on. In divers and sundry other places faro banks and roulette wheels were run openly—so openly, indeed, that a person could walk in from the sidewalk and see these banking games in full blast, there being no doors of restriction.

Professional gamblers from other States, especially from Michigan, Ohio, Illinois, Kentucky, Pennsylvania, Maryland, and particularly from the city of New York, came to Saratoga and openly violated and transgressed these laws during the past season. The local authorities took no action against it. Some of the prominent citizens of that county made an appeal to this Society, asking us to send officers there to get the evidence and have these men arrested. I was one of the men detailed for this work. I had with me one of my assistants, Mr. M. J. Sullivan.

We personally visited these places and saw the gambling games going on; visited the race track, where there were some fifteen or more places or booths occupied by gamblers; and among these gamblers thus openly violating the law was one Deputy Sheriff and two Constables from the town of Saratoga Springs.

I beg to present that we secured the most positive and absolute evidence of guilt against some twenty-eight or twenty-nine gamblers, twenty-three of whom were arrested and held for the action of the Grand Jury.

At the October term of the court at Ballston the witnesses were examined. Their testimony was taken down in writing and is now in the minutes of the Grand Jury. This evidence was not contradicted nor were the witnesses impeached in any way, and yet not a single bill of indictment was found against one of these gamblers, notwithstanding the absolute evidence of the guilt of the defendants, at least by two eyewitnesses in each case, and in some cases four and five witnesses.

While before the Grand Jury I was asked such questions as these: " Mr. Comstock, do you propose to pay the county for the expense of prosecuting these men in case we indict?" I replied: "No; I don't." "Will your Society pay the expense of prosecuting these men?" I replied that I submitted that the question was improper and that it had nothing whatever to do with the guilt or innocence of the defendants.

The Secretary of the Grand Jury informed me that he was a taxpayer in Saratoga, and that it would have very much to do with his verdict, for if they indicted these men it would cost the county $50,000 to try them. I said that I could not conceive such a thing was possible; but that, in that case, I submitted to the Grand Jury that that was a matter they had no right to consider. The Secretary said he "should consider it." And from my conversation with this gentleman, and with others on the Grand Jury, I am satisfied, beyond any question, that the Grand Jurors, or so many of them as voted not to find indictments, voted not to find them in the face of most absolute and positive evidence of guilt.

Mr. Foley, the then District Attorney, told me that he told the Grand Jury that "the evidence was full and absolute of the guilt of the defendants." I went to the presiding Judge and laid the facts before him, and he said that "if they did not find bills, the only thing to do was to bring the matter before the attention of the next Grand Jury." He also informed me that he had not been advised of the facts at all, and made no special charge to the Grand Jury concerning this particular evil.

I therefore beg to present to your Honor these facts, and in the in-

terest of law, order, and justice I beg to ask, if your Honor has any
doubt of my word, that you will examine the minutes of the last Grand
Jury in the cases, a list of which I present herewith. Our examination was taken down in writing and is very full. And if you find that
the statements I make are correct, and that there is absolute evidence
against these parties from at least two eye-witnesses, Mr. Sullivan and
myself, I respectfully ask that these matters may be brought before the
coming Grand Jury for such action as the evidence and the law
warrant.

With the list of names I append a brief of one or two cases showing
how these statutes have been construed in other courts, in order that
your Honor may have the facts before you concisely without being
obliged to take the time to look them up.

I have the honor to be,

With very great respect, sir,

Your obedient servant,

(Signed)   ANTHONY COMSTOCK,

Secretary.

There was enclosed a list of names in this letter of all
the cases named in the foregoing letter to Mr. Hamilton.

We were in hopes that these two communications would
result in rescuing the administration of justice from the
thraldom of the gamblers and secure indictments against
all of the guilty parties.   At this writing, however, *no witness has been called by the District Attorney,* and, so far as
known, no steps have thus far been taken to enforce the law
against these gamblers.

Whether any responsibility rests upon the District Attorney
or the courts of Saratoga County, this one thing is clear,
that the proprietors of faro banks, roulette tables, pool and
other gambling games of Saratoga—crimes of the grade of
felonies—have the power to say that the laws shall not
be enforced, and their word is law seemingly, so far as
the local authorities are concerned.

Let thoughtful citizens add together the power now
wielded by the lawless classes in Kings and Saratoga
Counties, and then say whether there is not in this at least

an alarm signal calling upon them to provide and fortify against the further encroachments of these crime-breeders.

The scourge of gambling is growing more and more odious to honest citizens. In two counties professional gamblers are stronger than law. Their influence is more potent than oath of office over officials. In face of the fact that the Legislature has year after year been solicited to repeal or change these laws, and as often has positively refused to make any change whatever, yet in two counties at least, professional gamblers, many of them non-residents of these counties, and in some instances non-residents of the State, have boldly asserted their intention to defy the law, and by their flagrant, persistent, and open violations of law have set at contempt the administration of justice, while they jeopardize the best interests of the community and the State.

Do gamblers own the State of New York? Are they stronger than law, courts, or justice?

General Catlin, in his very lame defence as to why he had not enforced the law against these pests, while he was District Attorney of Kings County, before the Bacon Investigating Committee swears:

"No preacher had ever preached against it up to that time and never did up to last fall, to my recollection, in 1886. No steps were taken in any way, shape, or manner by the so-called moral element of the city of Brooklyn to put a stop to this pool-selling business."

It will be remembered that in October last the clergymen of the city of Brooklyn inquired into the outrages in Kings County, and then made a presentment to the public. The latter part of that presentment is well worthy of consideration in this place. They say:

"The claim made both by General Catlin and by Mr. Ridgway, that in their failure to vigorously enforce the laws with respect to gambling they have had the tacit approval of the public, shows conclusively that part of the burden of responsibility for the miscarriage of justice rests with a community silent hitherto upon those matters, and indicates the necessity of explicit public utterance and decided action."

We now appeal to the public. The facts are before you. The correspondence will show how faithfully and with what fidelity the New York Society for the Suppression of Vice has brought the attention of the courts to the outrages against law and justice. Good legal evidence has been secured and placed in the hands of District Attorneys ; and notwithstanding all, the servants of the people, under solemn oaths of office to the contrary, as we submit has been clearly established in this record, have permitted the laws to be set aside and have failed to discharge their duty as public servants.

Is there not enough involved for the minister of the gospel to take public issue with these crimes and lend his voice and influence to the enforcement of law ? Are there not patriotic reasons enough involved to awaken every law-abiding citizen to the dangers that threaten the State ? Will it not be easier to overthrow these crimes and their advocates now, before they further corrupt our youth and lay hold upon the highest interests of our State with a death-grip equal to the rum power of the day, than it will be to allow them to go on corrupting courts, officials, and public servants until the State of New York shall be worse than the State of Louisiana is to-day under the corrupt influences of the Louisiana Lottery, and then attempt it ?

To turn over the State to a gang of merciless gamblers, and allow them to defy courts, violate laws, trample under foot justice, and treat with contempt the Legislature of the State, is to undermine the very foundations of our free institutions. It is destruction of equity, peace, and morals. It is against common right.

At Verne, Switzerland, there is a statue of a monster

13

devouring helpless children.   So this greedy monster, Gaming, is constantly wrecking the lives of those brought within
its reach, jeopardizing every public and private interest to
satisfy its greed for gain.

CHAPTER XII.

THE "IVES POOL BILL."

Since the foregoing pages of this book were written many important events concerning the gambling method of improving the breed of horses have passed into history.

Strange as it may seem, with the findings of the Ministers' Committee of October last, and of the Bacon Investigating Committee, both of which clearly demonstrated the utter lawlessness of the gambling fraternity, and with a full exposure of the facts concerning this lawlessness repeatedly laid before the public by the press of this State—in the face of all these facts stands one still more appalling, that the Ives Pool Bill was even a possibility, much less could become a law.

This law, under the pretence of restricting this evil, has practically condoned the past offences of gamblers who had been repeatedly indicted, while it legalizes the crimes which are the very root and essence of dishonesty and corruption. To legalize and sanction public gambling is to strike a death-blow at industrious habits. *It indorses dishonest practices.* To give the sanction of law to the dishonest practices of the pool gambler is to put a premium upon crime and sell out the morals of the community to the highest bidder.

The Ives Pool Bill was cunningly worded. It was speciously drawn so as to make it appear upon its face that its purpose was to provide a fund for the "improvement of cattle, sheep, and horses." No reader of this bill unless familiar with the provisions of Section 351 of the Penal Code would see anything in it to even arouse suspicion of its true character. The "nigger in the fence" is the suspension of Section 351. The bill as originally drawn proposed to suspend Section 351 of the Penal Code upon every race track in the State for twenty days each year. It also proposed to repeal all laws that in any way conflicted with its provisions.

This bill was rushed through the Assembly with a bare majority of two votes. It went over to the Senate, and on the 3d of May the Senate Judiciary Committee reported it to the Senate, refusing to wait until after a mass meeting that was to be held on that evening (May 3) in the Academy of Music, Brooklyn, could send delegates there to protest against its passage.

A grand mass meeting was held in the city of Brooklyn in the Academy, on the evening of May 3, 1886. The Academy of Music was filled. The platform was crowded with eminent men. The following protest was unanimously adopted, and at once sent to Senator Griswold at the Senate in Albany :

Whereas, A bill known as the Ives Pool Bill has passed the Assembly of the Legislature of the State of New York, and is now before the Senate for final passage ; and

Whereas, This bill proposes to abrogate, suspend, or repeal Section 351 of the Penal Code in the interest of combination, French and auction pools, and book-making, both upon horse-racing as well as upon elections ; and

Whereas, Well-known and professional gamblers have for years flagrantly, persistently, and openly violated existing laws, which crimes committed the Ives Pool Bill now proposes to condone, and to legalize the same hereafter upon every race course in the State ; and

Whereas, Embezzlements, defalcations, robberies, breaches of trust, thefts, intemperance, suicides, and murders are the result of gambling passions ; and

Whereas, Both in England and in America, under Common Law, it is held that a common gambling house, kept for lucre or gain, is *per se* a common nuisance, as it tends to draw together idle and evil-disposed persons, to corrupt their morals and ruin their fortunes ; and

Whereas, The scheme of pools as proposed to be legalized by the

Ives Pool Bill is one in which the public are to be invited to hazard small sums of money for the purpose of receiving as prizes larger sums, which has been decided by the Court of Appeals to be a lottery, and is therefore in violation of the Constitution of this State; and

Whereas, Section 7 of said bill will repeal all existing laws against lotteries and pool-selling; therefore

Resolved, That we, citizens of Brooklyn, in mass meeting assembled, this 3d day of May, 1887, in the city of Brooklyn, do enter this our most solemn protest against the passage of the Ives Pool Bill, or of any similar bill which proposes to legalize gambling of any kind in the State of New York.

Resolved, That a committee of five be appointed by the Chairman of this meeting to present this protest to the Senate at Albany, and to take such action as shall be necessary to defeat the passage of this bill.

Resolved, That copies of these resolutions, attested by the Chairman and Secretary of this meeting, be furnished to the press of New York and Brooklyn for publication.

Rev. T. DeWitt Talmage, D.D., Rev. Edward P. Ingersoll, D.D., H. D. Dumont, Esq., J. Warren Greene, Esq., and Hon. A. W. Tenny were appointed by this meeting a committee to go to Albany, and if possible to defeat this iniquitous measure. The next day this committee, accompanied by the Secretary of the New York Society for the Suppression of Vice, went to Albany. The next morning despatches were sent to Senator Griswold of Kings County, and largely through his efforts the measure was sent back to the Judiciary Committee of the Senate, and a hearing was had that afternoon. This resulted in the striking out of the "repeal" clause, and also in amending the bill so as to limit the racing between the 15th of May and the 15th of October each year, instead of the entire year, as the bill originally allowed. These amendments were found to be necessary as a compromise measure on behalf of the advocates of the bill in order to secure a report for the bill after our hearing. With these amendments the bill was reported to the Senate a few days afterwards.

May 12 the bill was brought up in the Senate and passed.

But in order to secure sufficient votes to pass it a still further compromise was found to be necessary, and upon the motion of Senator Parker, of Albany, the matter which now appears in Section 7 was added. With that compromise measure added the bill was passed, having just the requisite seventeen votes in the Senate necessary to pass it.

The following is a full text of the bill, together with the names of the members of the Assembly and Senate who voted for it, to wit:

AN ACT

Prescribing the period in each year during which and the terms under which racing may take place upon the grounds of associations incorporated for the purpose of improving the breed of horses, and suspending the operation of certain sections of the Penal Code.

The people of the State of New York, represented in Senate and Assembly, do enact as follows :—

Section 1. A tax of 5 per cent. upon the gross amounts of the receipts for admission on race days to race tracks or grounds on which racing is had, owned, leased, or conducted by a racing association incorporated under the laws of the State of New York for the purpose of improving the breed of horses, whether for the improvement of the thoroughbred or the trotting horse, shall be annually paid by such associations to the Comptroller of the State of New York within fifteen days after the 1st day of December in each year.

Sec. 2. It shall be the duty of the President or Treasurer of every association liable to be taxed, as provided in this act, to make a report in writing to the Comptroller annually, on or before the 15th day of November in each year, stating the amount of its gross receipts for admission to its race course on race day, which shall be duly verified by the oath of its treasurer.

Sec. 3. Whenever any such association shall neglect or refuse to make such report at the time prescribed in this act, the Comptroller is authorized to examine, or cause to be examined, its books and records, and to fix and determine the amount of tax due in pursuance of the provisions of this act. In case of the non-payment of the amount of tax so ascertained to be due, together with the expenses of such examination, for a period of thirty days after notice, any such association so in default, in addition thereto, shall be liable to pay to the State for each such omission or failure a sum not less than $500 nor more than $1000. The same may be sued for and recovered in the name of the people of the State in any court having competent jurisdiction by the Attorney General at the instance of the Comptroller. The Comptroller is also authorized and required to report any failure of any such association to make such report and to pay its tax to the Governor, who, if he shall be satisfied that such failure was intentional, shall thereupon direct the Attorney General to take proceedings in the name of the people of the State, to declare the charter of such association to be forfeited and its charter privileges at an end, and for such intentional failure the charter privileges, corporate rights, and franchises of every such association shall cease, end, and be determined.

Sec. 4. The number of days upon which races may be conducted upon any race track or ground is limited to thirty days in each year, and dur‑ ing that number of days only races shall be authorized and allowed up‑ on such tracks or grounds, during which time the same may be kept open for the admission of the public, subject to the conditions and limitations prescribed by the acts, or the several amendments thereto, under which the said associations were incorporated, and the provisions of Sections 351 and 352 of the Penal Code shall not apply to the grounds of such as‑ sociations as shall have complied with the provisions of Section 1 of this act during the number of days in each year during which the said races are hereby authorized. Such racing and pool-selling in this State shall be confined to the period between the 15th day of May and the 15th day of October in each year, and all pool selling shall be confined to the tracks where the races take place and on the days when the races take place.

Sec .5. The Comptroller shall issue to every racing association paying a tax under the provisions of this act a receipt for the same, and such receipt shall be presumptive evidence of such payment.

Sec. 6. All revenues which shall be received by the said Comptroller from the taxation prescribed in this act shall constitute a fund which shall be annually disbursed on behalf of the State for prizes for improv‑ ing the breed of cattle, sheep, and horses at the various county fairs throughout the State by the State Agricultural Society.

Sec. 7. Any person who shall engage in pool-selling at any time or place except as heretofore stated shall be guilty of a felony, and upon conviction shall be punished by imprisonment in the State Prison for a period not less than one nor more than five years.

Sec. 8. This act shall take effect immediately.

ASSEMBLYMEN.

Yeas—Messrs. Bates, Baucus, Berry, Bonnington, Brennan, Bulkley, Burke, Bush, Cantor, Collins, Conover, Cutler, Dalton Dickey, Evans, Farrell, Finn, Fitch, Giese, Goerss, Gorman, Graham, Greene, Grippin, Guenther, Hagan, Haggerty, Hayes, G. H. Henry, L. S. Henry, Hill, Hines, Hornidge, Ives, Kenney, Kunzenman, Langbein, Longley, Mabie, Manville, Martin, Mase, Maurer, Maxwell, McAdam, McCann, McCarthy, McIntyre, McLaughlin, McMahon, Moore, Mulry, Newton, Power, Prime, Reeves, Reitz, Ryan, Seaver, Shea, Sheehan, Charles Smith, Martin A. Smith, Robert H. Smith, Sullivan, Wafer, Wemple Winne—69.

SENATORS.

Yeas—Messrs. Cogeshall, Cullen, Daly, Dunham, Fagan, Hoysradt, McMillan, Murphy, Nelson, Parker, Pierce, Plunkitt, Raines, Reilly, Traphagen, Wemple, Worth—17.

A hearing was had before the Governor on the 23d of May, when a large delegation from Brooklyn and other places appeared before him. Rev. Dr. Talmage, of Brooklyn, Rev. Dr. MacArthur, of New York, and other eminent gentlemen appeared before the Governor to urge him to veto this bill. Telegrams and letters were received in large numbers from representative men, ministers and eminent citizens, from all parts of the State. Churches of all denominations either sent delegates or their protests against the bill, and their demand was that " *the bill be vetoed.*" A brief was filed with the Governor showing that the bill was unconstitutional. Yet, notwithstanding all, on the 25th of May, at midnight, this bill became law, because David B. Hill's ear was deaf to the appeals of the moral and religious elements of this State.

After the hearing, and before the bill became law, the following circular was sent out in the city of New York, predicated, as will be seen, upon the assurance of the gamblers that the Governor would permit the bill to become law. This circular was telegraphed in full to Governor Hill, showing him exactly how the evil was to be spread over the city, and continued, if the crimes which the Legislature had declared to be FELONIES by their amendment should go into effect. The circular read as follows:

SIR:—The selling of pools and book-making within the gates of the race tracks of this State having been legalized by recent legislative enactment, it is certain that those who desire to invest must either themselves visit the course or have their business transacted by others.

In view of the frequent impracticability of the former alternative, the following proposition is respectfully submitted for your consideration:

I will call at your office every morning, take your order, and place your money at the track in any manner you desire, all transactions to be considered strictly confidential.

The charges will be very moderate—5 per cent. on sums of $30 or less; $1.50 on all sums between $30 and $60, and $3 for all sums from $60 to $500. It will be seen that the cost of placing the lowest sum at the track will be less than the actual expense of going to the track for the purpose, and far below what it would cost (considering the difference in the odds obtained) to place it in the city, even if such a thing were possible.

This circular will be followed by a personal call, at which time, should you desire to take advantage of this convenient arrangement, further particulars and satisfactory guarantee as to responsibility will be furnished.

Respectfully,

A. H. MILLS.

26 North William Street, City.

The New York *Herald*, in announcing the action of the Governor the day following, says:

"In memoranda filed with the Secretary of State the Governor gives the following reasons why he pursued the course he has in disposing of this important measure:"

FIVE REASONS.

First—The bill involves no constitutional question.

Second—It involves no political question about which parties are divided.

Third—It had a full, fair, and deliberate discussion in both houses and in the public press for weeks before its passage in the Legislature.

Fourth—It presents a question upon which public sentiment seems to be greatly divided and one peculiarly within the province of the Legislature to determine.

Fifth—It regulates and restrains the selling of pools by permitting such sales during a limited period and at certain places only, and by prohibiting, under increased penalties, such sales at all other times and places, and imposes for the privilege a license fee or tax which is uniform throughout the State.

*   *   *   *   *   *   *   *   *   *   *   *

DAVID B. HILL.

Governor Hill declares " the bill involves no constitutional question." There are two sides to this question. To differ from him is the right of those who think more of morals than of votes. Look a moment at the other side of this constitutional question.

There are two points which should be especially emphasized in this connection.

First, Article III. of the Constitution of this State provides that

" No act shall be passed which shall provide that any existing law, or any part thereof, shall be made or deemed a part of said act, or which shall enact that any existing law, or any part thereof, shall be applicable, except by inserting it in such act."—(Art. III., Sec. 17, Constitution, 1875.)

Observe particularly two things under this head :

First. The Ives Pool Bill suspends Section 351 of the Penal Code without setting out the section in the bill, or naming it in its title.

Second. Section 7 of the Ives bill raises one of the many crimes prohibited in Section 351 —*pool-gambling* — to the grade of a felony, but is silent as to all the others, except to permit them on race courses.

Third. Nothing in its title indicates that the Ives Pool Bill is to increase the penalties of Section 351 or change the grade of the crimes prohibited by it.

Fourth. The Ives bill pretends to say that offenders against Section 351, Penal Code, outside of a race course, are to be treated as felons, and are liable to " not less than one year nor more than five years' imprisonment," if they sell pools, and yet Section 351 is not inserted in the bill, as is required by Section 17 of Article III. of the Constitution.

In the eager haste to get the bill through the Senate they have failed to amend the title of the bill, and have inserted into a law " prescribing the period in each year during which and the terms under which racing may take place upon the grounds of associations incorporated for the purpose of improving the breed of horses, and suspending the operations of certain sections of the Penal Code," an amendment to a penal statute, changing the crimes prohibit_ ed from misdemeanors to felonies, and this too without inserting the section of the Penal Code particularly affected in the act.

Governor Hill says that it does not violate the Constitution·

Will he say that such jumbled up legislation does not violate the spirit as well as the letter of Article III. sufficiently to have made a veto his imperative duty?

Let thinking people answer for him.

Why should the one crime of pool-selling be singled out and made the item of special penalties, and the other crimes, to wit, the keeping, occupying, or using of a room, tent, tenement, booth, or building, or part thereof, with paraphernalia for recording or registering bets or wagers, not be included in the same category?

Were there not good, sound reasons in these inconsistencies for a veto?

But consider the second point.

"French pool, " which is prohibited by Section 351, and allowed by the Ives bill, is *a lottery,* and has so been declared by the courts in this country and England.

If French pool is a lottery, then this law which permits it is in conflict with the Constitution again, where it says:

"Nor shall any lottery hereafter be authorized, or any sale of lottery tickets allowed, within this State."—(Article I., Section 10, Constitution, 1881.)

The Ives bill permits tickets to be sold in French pool. These tickets are lottery tickets within the definitions of all our courts.

Let the reader now carefully consider two things under his subject:

First, get a clear understanding of what French pool is; then apply the definitions of a lottery, as laid down by the authorities, to it.

The question under discussion, then, is: Is the system of pool-selling which the Ives Pool Bill authorizes and permits for thirty days each year, upon each and every race track in the State, in conflict with the prohibition of the Constitution of the State of New York?

In this connection it is of first importance to clearly understand what the Ives Pool Bill permits and what French pool is. This bill allows the keeping of paraphernalia upon every race track in the State during a period of thirty days each year for the purpose of selling "French pools," "auction pools," and "combination pools" and for "recording bets and wagers," not only "upon the result of any trial or contest of skill, speed, or power of endurance between horses," but also "upon the result of any trial or contest of skill, speed, or power of endurance between *men*." It also allows pools to be sold and bets and wagers recorded upon the "result of any political nomination, appointment, or election."

We have not to deal in this discussion with book-making, which is known in the law as "recording bets and wagers," but simply with "French pools."

To make it clear to the reader's mind that "French pool" is a lottery, let me show the practical working of "French pool." Let it be premised that there are ten horses to run in a certain race. The names of these horses are publicly displayed upon a blackboard, or otherwise, with a number opposite each name, which number each horse is known by. Tickets are sold by the pool-seller with numbers corresponding to those opposite the names of each horse. These tickets are usually sold at $5 each, and entitle the holder to a "share, chance, or interest" of whatever moneys remain in the pool after the pool-seller deducts his commission of five per cent. This amount can only be determined at the close of the race or when the sale of tickets ceases : and the tickets which draw prizes are only those sold upon the winning horse. The amount to be distributed by chance, or upon the contingency of the race, let it be supposed, is $1000. After the race is run the pool-seller deducts his commission from this amount. He then divides the pool into as many shares as there are tickets sold on the winning horse. Each ticket sold on the race represents a share, chance, or interest in the money in the pool, and all have an even chance of winning a prize. I omitted to state that as each ticket is sold it is recorded opposite the name and number of the horse upon which it is sold, upon an instrument designed for that purpose, or else upon a blackboard.

Two hundred tickets must be sold to make up the $1000 purse which is to be distributed as prizes. It is the chance of winning a part of this for which ticket buyers pay their $5. Suppose ten of these tickets are sold upon the winning horse, the ten persons who have paid $5 for the chance receive each one-tenth of the pool less the pool-seller's commission, while the 190 others lose their money, although the 190 losers have each paid $5 for the *chance* of winning a prize, and until the lot was cast had an even chance with the others of winning a prize.

First, take the definition of a lottery as it is laid down in the Penal Code :

" Section 323. A lottery is a scheme for the distribution of property by chance among persons who have paid or agreed to pay a valuable consideration for the chance, whether called a lottery, raffle, gift enterprise, or *by some other name*."—(Sec. 323, Penal Code, p. 135. People *vs*. C. D. J. Noelke, 94 N. Y. R., 141.)

Now note the legal definitions of a lottery, as laid down by our Court of Appeals and other high courts.

The Court of Appeals has defined a lottery in a case where the defendant was indicted for selling a lottery ticket, and yet where the defence was set up that it was not in form a lottery, but rather simply a bet or wager that certain numbers would appear in a list to be drawn at a certain time. The evidence showed that the defendant made a bet that certain numbers would appear in a list that were to be drawn in a certain drawing then about to take place. The Court says :

" The word 'lottery' has no technical legal meaning. It must be construed in the popular sense, and with a view of remedying the mischief intended to be prevented.

" It is defined by Webster as a 'scheme for the distribution of prizes by chance, or the distribution itself ; ' and he defines ' lot ' as that which ' causes, falls, or happens ; that which in human speech is called chance, fortune, hazard.'

" Worcester defines a lottery as 'a hazard in which small sums are ventured for the chance of obtaining a greater value.'

" The language of Folger, J., in 56 N. Y., 424, may be adopted as a final result of the accepted definitions :

" ' Where a pecuniary consideration is paid, and it is to be determined by lot or chance, according to some scheme held out to the public, what and how much he who pays the money is to have for it, that is a lottery.' "—(Wilkinson *vs*. Gill, 74 N. Y., 66.)

Again the Court of Appeals says, in reference to form :

" The Courts have uniformly looked beyond the mere form or device of the transaction, and sought out and suppressed the substance itself."

—(Govs. of Almshouse *vs.* American Art Union, 7 N. Y., 228. Hull *vs.* Ruggles, 56 N. Y., 424.)

" It is not necessary that there should be an organized institution, or that the scheme should be called a lottery. It matters not by what name it is called or what terms are used. . . . It is said that the transaction is a wager or bet that certain numbers will draw, and is therefore not a lottery. This does not follow.

"Every lottery has the characteristics of a wager or bet. . . . A lottery, or game of device in the nature of a lottery, is not excluded from the operations of the statute because it also partakes of the nature of a wager."—(74 N. Y., 66, 67. People *vs.* Noelke, 94 N. Y., 141.)

Says the Court of Appeals again :

" Any game, or device of chance in the nature of a lottery, is within the prohibition of the statutes against lotteries."—(Wilkinson *vs.* Gill., 74 N. Y., 63.)

In defining a " lottery ticket " Chief Justice Bronson says :

" A ticket need not be in the form of a written contract or agreement. It may be any sign, symbol, or memoranda of the holder's interest in the lottery.—(People *vs.* Taylor, 3 Denio, 100. Citing Com. *vs.* Chubb, 5 Randolph, Va., 715. Com. *vs.* Pollard, Thatcher's Crim. C., 280.)

Again a lottery is defined as follows :

" So long as the event could not be predicted by the party concerned it would be uncertain and dependent upon chance in the only sense which the law has to take into account."—(Com. *vs.* Thatcher, 93 Mass., 83. Com. *vs.* Wright, 137 Mass., 251. State *vs.* Clark, 33 N. H., 329.)

But it is claimed that pool-selling is a harmless amusement. Note what the Court of Appeals of this State says, in speaking of this " Constitutional prohibition against lotteries," even though the objects were innocent. In the celebrated case of the Govs. of the Almshouse of New York *vs.* The American Art Union, 7 N. Y., Reports 239, 241, the Court says :

" The prohibition was not aimed at the objects for which lotteries had
been authorized, but at that particular mode of accomplishing such objects. It was founded on the moral principle that evil should not be
done that good might follow, and upon the more cogent practical reason that the evil consequent on this pernicious kind of gambling greatly
overbalanced in the aggregate any good likely to result from it."

In speaking of the " universal passion for playing at games
of chance," in this same case the Court says :

" The indulgence of this passion was precisely what the Constitution
intended to repress and prohibit.
" The Constitution took away from the Legislature the power of determining whether this or any other lottery was of good or evil tendency.
If it were to be admitted that the scheme is entirely harmless in its consequences, it would form no ground for making it by judicial const uc-
tion "(or otherwise) " an exception to the general and absolute constitu
tional prohibition."

In this connection let it be observed that a ticket
sold in any scheme called a lottery is as much a bet that
the number upon that ticket will draw a prize as the $5 bet
upon the number opposite the name of the horse in French
pool is a bet that that particular horse or that particular
number will win.

Note what the Court of Appeals says of the element of
chance in pool-selling :

" Each party gets a chance of gain from others, and takes a risk of
loss of his own to them."—(Harris vs. White, 81 N. Y., 539.)

Is not this the very essential of a lottery ? Is it not true
in every lottery ? But if this argument shall go for naught,
in New Jersey the highest court there has declared " auction
pool," " French pool," and " combination pool " upon horse
races "LOTTERIES."   In England French pool is held to
be a game of chance, as will be seen further on ; also a lottery.

In the celebrated case of " State of New Jersey vs. Lovell "
(one of the boss pool-sellers of the State of New York), the

defendant was indicted for " setting up, opening, and making a certain lottery, and for selling a lottery ticket therein." Upon the trial it was shown that his offence was the selling of pools upon horse races, as named above.

The Court cited the definition of a lottery as given in Hull *vs.* Ruggles, 56 N. Y., 424 (since re-affirmed in Wilkinson *vs.* Gill, 74 N. Y., and more recently approved in People *vs.* Noelke, 94, N. Y.), and then said :

" The scheme of pools set up by the defendant was one in which the public were to be invited to hazard small sums of money for the purpose of receiving as prizes larger sums.

" But it was insisted on behalf of the defendant that, whether the person hazarding the small sum was to receive a larger one or not depended not upon chance, but upon his own good or bad judgment in selecting the horse upon which he placed his bet."

The Court says in answer to this :

" The physical condition of the horse and his rider, the fastenings of his shoes, the honesty of purpose that actuates his rider and owner in running him, the state of the weather and the track, and these circumstances in the case of every horse that runs against him, are all matters about which the judgment of the outside bettor can avail him no more than the arithmetical calculations of chance can avail the dice thrower.

" There is, however, aside from the result of the race, another element of chance in these games, which is clearly pointed out in Tollett *vs.* Thomas, L. R. 6, Q. B. 514, and that is the element which determines what the winner is to gain. That element in the ' auction pool ' depends upon how much others may bet against him, and in the ' French pool ' and ' combination pool ' upon how many others may bet as he does. None of the bettors, save the last one, can possibly learn these matters. I need not repeat what is said in the case cited as to these ingredients making the transaction a game of chance."

And then concludes as follows in reference to the intent of the act for the suppression of lotteries :

" Having a direct tendency to produce those pernicious mischiefs in a community which the act for the suppression of lotteries was intended to prevent."—(State *vs.* Lovell, 39 Vroom, 272.)

14

Does not this evil come within the spirit of the constitutional prohibition against lotteries sufficient to have required and justified a veto ?

In the above case of Tollett *vs.* Thomas, Thomas had been convicted by two judges for selling tickets in what was then called "*Pari Mutuel*," being precisely the same as " French pool."

It came up upon appeal before the Queen's Bench, Lord Chief Justice Cockburn presiding. There were two questions brought before this court for their decision.

" I. Is the machine (for registering the tickets sold) an instrument of gaming ?

" II. Is the game on which the wagering took place, under the circumstances stated, *a game of chance ?* "

Says this high court :

"Whether a horse race be in itself a game of chance or not, we can entertain no doubt that, if some additional element of chance be introduced, the wagering on a horse race may be converted into a game of chance. Thus, to use a familiar illustration, a lottery in which each individual draws a particular horse, on the success of which the winning of the stakes depends, would, we cannot doubt, constitute as between the parties to such a lottery a game of chance. In the present instance, an element of chance is introduced which, though not having any reference to the main event—namely, the result of the race in the winning of a particular horse—is yet essential to making the wager laid upon the winning horse profitable to the bettor.

" The winning of the horse betted upon is of course the primary condition of the wager being won ; but whether the winning of the wager shall be productive of any profit to the winner, and more especially what the amount of that profit shall be, depends on the state of the betting with reference to the number of bets laid on or against the winning horse—a state of things fluctuating from one minute to another throughout the duration of the betting.

" Now this being something wholly independent of the issue of the race as well as of the will and judgment of the winner, depending as it does on the will or caprice of the other persons betting, is a matter obviously of *uncertainty and chance* to the individual bettor, more especially in the earlier stages of betting.

"There being, then, this *element of chance* in the transaction among the parties betting, we think it may properly be termed, as amongst them, a game of chance."—(L. R. 6, G. B., 521.)

Query: Is not French pool a lottery, and within the letter and spirit of the constitution of the State of New York?

Would a veto against the Ives Pool Bill have been misplaced?

Speaking of the demoralization of this class of gambling, particularly "lotteries," the Supreme Court of the United States, in a recent case, says :

" That lotteries are demoralizing in their effects, no matter how carefully regulated, cannot in the opinion of this court be doubted. Experience has shown that the common forms of gambling are partially innocuous when placed in contact with the wide-spread pestilence of lotteries. The lottery infests the whole community, enters every home, preys upon the hard earnings of the poor, and it plunders the ignorant and simple."—(Stone *vs.* State of Miss., 11 Otto. 818. Phalen *vs.* Va. 8 Howard, 163, 168.)

Place beside these words of wisdom of the highest court of this nation those words of equal weight and wisdom as quoted from that celebrated jurist, Judge Catron, as given in the foregoing pages of this book, and then say whether or no the operating of gambling paraphernalia in the midst of thronged multitudes, by trained and professional gamblers, is not an element of danger that this State ought to rise up against at once and crush out !

From the first introduction of the Ives Pool Bill, the gambling fraternity have acted upon an implied understanding that their pool bill was to become law. For instance, the day it became law the New York *World* contained the following concerning the opening of the Brooklyn Jockey Club race track, which shows that their plans were completed and that the gamblers stood ready to move upon the public as soon as the ten days required by law had expired in which this bill should become law, unless the Governor vetoea it. Says the *World*, May 26, 1887 :—

" The immense betting pavilion was naturally a scene of great animation between each of the races, and the betting stands were besieged by the speculators, but there was no demonstration and a placid serenity prevailed at the enjoyed immunity from police espionage.

" The book-making firms were on hand early. There were sixty of them, and they quickly drew forth their betting booths. Much surprise was manifested at the absence of Kelly and Bliss from the arena, and many were the questions asked as to the reason of their absence. On inquiry it was ascertained that the firm was affluent enough to take a rest and that Mr. Kelly had assumed a retiring disposition. However, there were enough to supply the market, and the sixty stands were occupied by the following firms :

No.		No.	
1.	Marshall & Co.	27.	Appleby & Johnson.
2.	A. M. Burton & Co.	28.	Murray & Co.
3.	J. Nathan.	29.	C. H. Thompson.
4.	Appleby & Johnson	30.	E. Croker.
5.	R. Hughes & Co.	31.	O. P. Keyes & Co.
6.	C. Heinman & Co.	32.	Straus & Co.
7.	J. L. Anderson & Co.	33.	Gale & Co.
8.	Worden & Co.	34.	G. Walbaum.
9.	Swatto & Co.	35.	Emery & Co.
10.	Corbett & Co.	36.	Ridge Levien.
11.	Irving & Co.	37.	W. J. Conner.
12.	Charles Davis.	38.	Spitz & Co.
13.	Appleby & Johnson.	39.	Cridge & Co.
14.	Eaton & Co.	40.	Henry Stedeker.
15.	Kirk & Co.	41.	Charles Reed.
16.	Michaels & Co.	42.	A. Anderson & Co.
17.	Spencer & Co.	43.	J. J. Gleason.
18.	McCloud & Mahoney.	44.	Downey & Co.
19.	Frank & Co.	45.	Hawkins & Co.
20.	P. Pappcheim.	46.	Hamell & Co.
21.	Mahoney & Co.	47.	Enright & Co.
22.	J. Hackett & Co.	48.	J. Shipsey.
23.	De Lacey & Co.	49.	J. K. Lane & Co.
24.	Medinger Bros.	50.	Joe Cotton.
25.	Shipsey Bros.	51.	John Daly & Co.
26.	E. T. Beaman.	52.	J. E. McDonnell.

53. Dimond & Co.	57. Sutton & Co.
54. Gamble & Co.	58. Arthur Hackett & Co.
55. Dexter & Co.	59. G. H. McCabe.
56. Shaw & Co.	60. Philip Daly & Co.

May 31 the Jerome Park races opened at Jerome Park, and the New York *World* further says that "the betting arrangements were under the responsible charge of Messrs. Kelly and Bliss, and early in the day the following firms drew stands as follows," presenting the list of the sixty pool-sellers named above. It is fair to say that the Brooklyn and Jerome Park Jockey Club each received at least $6000 rental each day from these sixty gambling booths. As these professional gamblers can have thirty days of gambling at Sheepshead Bay, thirty days at Jerome Park, and thirty days more at the Brooklyn Jockey Club track, it is safe to say that their receipts on these three race tracks of money drawn from the pocket of the public and paid over to the jockey clubs alone amounts to $540,000 during these ninety days on these three tracks, and all for " improving the breed of horses." A tax of $540,000 levied upon the thoughtless public in order that the jockey clubs may race horses and afford gamblers an opportunity to rob the people to the utmost of their ability ! The $540,000 is only a fractional part of the receipts of the sixty gamblers.

The Legislature did one thing in connection with the passage of this bill that was commendable, and it is the only respectable thing about the whole matter ; and that was when they branded one of these robbery schemes—pool gambling—a felony. But look at the inconsistency of declaring a crime a felony, and then setting up a board fence and saying to professional gamblers : " If you will come over on the inside of our fence you may commit these felonies every day from the fifteenth of May to the fifteenth of October each year, provided you change your base of operations every thirty days."

This is what Governor Hill says " regulates and restrains the selling of pools by permitting such sales during the limited period," etc. The history of gambling from the earliest inception of legislation against it down to the present time presents a record most disgraceful and demoralizing. Of all the shameful things that have ever come upon the State of New York this is the worst—to legalize the acts of professional gamblers, many of whom are non-residents of this State, while others are ex-convicts and others still under suspension of sentence. And to permit them to rob the public under authority of law is the most iniquitous and outrageous of all.

The advocates of this bill would never have presumed to ask such men as William H. Seward, John A. Dix, Alonzo B. Cornell, or Grover Cleveland, when they were in charge of the State, to consent that such a blot as this law is should be put upon the State of New York. No man who knew either of these men would have had the hardihood to ask their consent to a measure as iniquitous as this.

Like the heathen mother who throws her babe into the Ganges to be devoured by the crocodiles which line the banks of that river, so these legislators who voted for this infamous law have practically taken our young men just starting in life and thrown them into the rapacious maw of the gambling fraternity, and made it *legal* for these crime-breeders to prey upon them, destroying their usefulness and their integrity.

With one vote the Legislature provides a law to punish a thief, and with the other says to the professional gambler: " It shall be legitimate for you to allure young men to dishonesty, and if they are ruined through your insidious temptations and influences, we will punish them and protect you."

Of the influences which helped to make this measure a

law the New York *World*, which advocated the bill with much zeal before its passage, June 3, 1887, says:—

DUPED BY THE LOBBYISTS.

ASSEMBLYMEN WHO CONFIDED IN THEM NOW NURSING
THEIR WRATH.

Money Promised for Legislative Votes Not on Hand when Called For—Threats Reaching Into Next Session.

ALBANY, June 2.—There is weeping and wailing and mutterings of wrath among members of the last Assembly. There is joy, exultation and profit among members of the Third House. Having for five months defeated the wishes of the people in legislation, members of the Assembly have just realized that they in return have been deplorably tricked by the lobby. The confiding and virtuous assemblyman has been duped by the shrewd and unscrupulous lobbyist. During the past session a constant source of amusement was afforded by the rivalry between the Kenmore gang and the Delavan House gang.

* * * * * * * * * * * *

The difference between the two gangs was as great as their respective methods. The Kenmore gang were satisfied with ·promises, and paid them out liberally and, as the result shows, by no means satisfactorily. The Delavan House sports played for spot cash, or no sale. To the Kenmore horde was allotted the cable scheme, the scheme to take $1,000,000 out of the State Treasury under the guise that it was a tax upon widows and orphans, the Grooved-Rail Bill, and the Ives Pool Bill. There were millions in these jobs. The average price offered for votes was $250. The gentlemen who have had their eye-teeth cut in dealing with legislative lobbyists insisted that the money should be paid down before the vote was cast. Their terms were agreed ·to. Other gentlemen who were satisfied to depend upon promises were contented to wait until final adjournment. These are the men who in New York City, in Albany, and in the State at large are tearing their hair, muttering their wrath, and threatening vengeance upon the lobbyists who have sold them out. There is a number of them.

It was given out last Thursday that members whose services had not been paid for would receive their compensation on Friday or Saturday. This compensation was placed as follows on the following bills : The Pool Bill, city members, $750; rural statesmen, $500. It is almost unnecessary to say that many patriotic statesmen lent their services to the corporations who were backing these schemes for the money that was in them.

Comments are needless.

It was urged as an argument in favor of the Ives bill that "millionaires favored it." Millions of money cannot of itself build up a noble character. A few dollars misappropriated can blast one instantly for all time. The youth who have plenty of money to gratify their appetites and passions are usually not the best examples nor the purest or noblest characters. They may, by a lavish expenditure of money, cast a glamour over their loose and sinful living and find apologists for their wicked ways, but this does not insure noble men for the future. It is men of sterling character that this age lacks. The future demands true men. *We need men*—manly men, men who are clean, honest, true, and noble in thought, word, and deed, whether they have a dollar in their pockets or not. It is character, not money; it is morals, not horses ; it is worth, not popular favor, that the State must look to in the future for support and defence.

It is claimed that this system of "improving the breed of horses" is necessary for the amusement of the people. History is full of the records of monsters who have amused the people by throwing human victims into the arena to be devoured by wild beasts. When such deeds shall receive the plaudit of approval from civilized nations it will be time enough to give a word of indorsement to schemes the very operation of which the experience of all ages declares to be against public morals and common right.

The question is : Have gamblers more control in this State than moral and religious people have ? If not, then for the sake of public morals, common honesty, public policy, and for the preservation of the institutions of free government, let the ballot box speak next Fall. Let honest men be elected and a demand made on every side that this iniquitous measure be repealed, and that Section '351 of the Code be amended so as to make the crimes contained in it Felonies everywhere; and make the penalty for non-enforcement of that law not only prompt removal from office, but barring forever from holding any office of trust any official who fails to do his duty.

Public morals and public order ought not to be sacrificed for the sake of the gambling fraternity or any profits or contribution that may be made by them to political parties.

May, 1887, must go down into history as the time when the State of New York was sold out to gamblers. This little book is an earnest and emphatic protest against the further carrying out of this contract made between politicians on one side and gamblers on the other. This contract was so iniquitous that the Governor of the State had not the courage to put his signature to it. Neither had he the wisdom and patriotism to veto it. This compact ought to be declared void, because it embodies in it principles that are destructive of public morals, good order, public policy, and common honesty.

It is the indifference of professional Christian men to the encroachments of evils flowing from rum, gambling, and a licentious and criminal press that makes many evils which prey upon the community possible. The religious press has not taken that bold, persistent, uncompromising position against these flagrant crimes which it ought to have taken. There is too much temporizing with these destructive elements on the part of good men. Politicians have sold themselves out in many cases to the criminal element, and political bosses are little less than bribe-takers, as it is notorious that the protection of these crimes is the pap upon which they fatten. It was the silence of good men that gave tacit consent to the passage of the Ives Pool Bill. The opposition came too late to avail against its passage. Church members who frequent the race course and patronize the betting ring do not heed the command : "Come out and be ye separate. Touch not the unclean thing." They are not governed by : " Ye cannot serve God and mammon." Every man should feel that the responsibility of checking these evils lies c. rectly at his door. There must be individual action. Let every good man rally around the standard of right, equity, and justice, strike down the robbers of the poor, raise voice and hand against the further encroachments of these monster evils, and cease not his activity until our State is reclaimed from the thraldom of dishonesty, intemperance, and uncleanness, and the power of the gambling fraternity. Let the war-cry be: "Down with the bosses who foster and protect crime of any kind." Let politicians who are mean enough to take blood-money, or blackmail the criminal class, feel that they cannot command or receive the votes of moral and upright citizens. Let the line be drawn upon the side of temperance, honesty, and moral purity, and let these virtues be cultivated, encouraged, and crowned with that fear of God which maketh rich and addeth no sorrow thereto.

www.ingramcontent.com/pod-product-compliance
Lightning Source LLC
Chambersburg PA
CBHW030318270326